Jeremiah and Lamentations

"I will put My law in their minds and write it on their hearts. I will be their God, and they will be My people."

Jeremiah 31:33

Revised from material by Daniel E. Poellet
Edited by Edward Engelbrecht

CONCORDIA PUBLISHING HOUSE • SAINT LOUIS

Contents

History	Date (B.C.)	Jeremiah
Josiah	640–609	Jeremiah's call (626), 1:2–19
Josiah's reformation	621	First attempts on life, 11:18–12:6
Fall of Nineveh	612	
Battle of Megiddo, Josiah killed	609	
Jehoahaz, deported to Egypt	609	Brief lament over Jehoahaz, 22:10–12
Jehoiakim	609–598	Arrested and saved, 26:7–24
Battle of Carchemish, Babylon defeats Egypt	605	Arrested, beaten, in stocks, 19:14–20:6 The scroll burned and replaced, ch. 36
Jehoiachin	598–597	
First deportation to Babylon	597	
Zedekiah	597–586	
Siege of Jerusalem begins (Nebuchadnezzar)	589	Urges submission to Babylon, ch. 27 Consulted by Zedekiah, 21:1–10; 37:1–10 Imprisoned, 37:11–21 Cistern experience, ch. 38
Fall of Jerusalem Second deportation to Babylon	586	In Mizpah, 39:1–40:6
Gedaliah governor	586–582	To Egypt, 43:1–7
Gedaliah assassinated Third deportation to Babylon	582	

An Outline of Jeremiah

The Book of Jeremiah divides into three major sections: (1) Prophecies, (2) Jeremiah's Struggles, and (3) Judgments. Jeremiah or his scribe arranged the material topically, not chronologically. (E.g., early in his ministry Jeremiah prophesied about the Babylonian exile. The prophecy appears with similar prophecies in chapters 25–29.)

Prophecies (chapters 1–25)

Jeremiah's Struggles (36–45)

Judgments against the Nations (46–52)

An Outline of Lamentations

Lamentations divides simply into five "laments" or poems of mourning.

Introduction

When the Book of Jeremiah first appeared, it was cut in pieces and burned. It was rewritten and is now more than twenty-five hundred years old. Jeremiah's prophecy is long, longer than all the biblical books except Psalms. Jeremiah's writings are difficult to study, for they have many passages of grief and tragedy. Yet, God wants you to study these books and treasure their message. As you study the writings of Jeremiah—his prophecy and his lament—may the Lord richly bless you.

There are about forty direct and indirect references to Jeremiah's writings in the New Testament. Half of them occur in the Revelation to St. John, which compares the Old Testament kingdom of Babylon with the kingdom of Satan. Special passages in this study will help you see Jeremiah's influence on the New Testament and his relationship to the Messiah, Jesus of Nazareth.

Lesson 1

The Prophet's Work

"In the past God spoke to our forefathers through the prophets at many times and in various ways," states the Book of Hebrews (1:1). One of these prophets was Jeremiah. To understand the man and his message, we need to know just what God called an Old Testament prophet to do.

Today, the word *prophet* has come to mean many things. We think of a prophet as one who predicts the future. We associate prophets with reform movements in society and religion. We believe them to be gifted teachers and spiritual leaders. Even in the language of the Scriptures the word *prophet* is applied to men of various personalities, behaviors, and skills.

1. What use of the word *prophet* is illustrated in each of the following passages?

1 Kings 18:22
1 Samuel 9:3–21
1 Samuel 19:18–24
2 Kings 5:1–14
1 Kings 22:13–14
Luke 7:16
Matthew 7:15
Matthew 26:68

These passages have shown that even in Scripture itself, *prophet* can mean various things. But the word is used also in a specific and restricted way. When the New Testament repeatedly speaks of "the Law or the Prophets" (e.g., Matthew 5:17), it has reference to a specific group of men and their message to the people of Israel. These were men called by God to "proclaim," to announce to the people of the Old Covenant the revelations He gave them. Their work was not primarily to *foretell*, but to *forthtell*. They were preachers, even though many of them wrote their message. Many prophetic messages are preserved in that body of Old Testament literature known as the prophetic books.

2. Page through the prophetic books in your Bible (Isaiah through Malachi). Can you detect why the first four (Isaiah, Jeremiah, Ezekiel, and Daniel) are called "major" prophets? What makes the other books "minor"?

The Prophets' Task

The prophets spoke for God. They proclaimed His counsel and will. They applied the promises and threats of God to the people of their time, kept the Law, and pointed to the coming Messiah as the fulfillment of the Law. In this task they were extensions of God Himself—not mechanical mouthpieces, but living, conscious, willing, and involved instruments of God who proclaimed what they themselves had received from Him.

3. Discuss what challenges might accompany "speaking for God." Read Deuteronomy 6:6–7 and Psalm 145:4–6. How are these prophetic challenges your challenges as well?

Methods of Proclamation

A prophet used different methods of proclamation. Most often he directly introduced his message in speech or writing with the phrase "The word of the LORD" or "This is what the LORD says" (e.g., Isaiah 38:4; 45:18). Another method was for the prophet to describe what he had seen in a vision or a dream (e.g., Daniel 7:1). A third method was the symbolic act, in which the prophet put into personal action the message that God wanted His people to know about themselves or their future (e.g., Ezekiel 4:1–4).

4. State which method of proclamation is illustrated in each of the following passages: Jeremiah 1:9; 13:1–9; 24:1–7.

History of Prophetic Activity

The first scriptural use of the word *prophet* is in a description of Abraham (Genesis 20:7). Later, God commissioned Moses and Aaron as messengers to the pharaoh of Egypt (Exodus 7:1–2). Then, in the time of Samuel, about 1100 B.C., the prophetic "office" was established as an institution of God in Israel (1 Samuel 3:19–21). Other individuals rose to succeed Samuel in the prophetic ministry, such as Elijah (1 Kings 17) and Elisha (2 Kings 2). There also seem to have been schools of the prophets, for the preparation of young men for this service (2 Kings 9:1–3).

These earlier prophets apparently had a somewhat limited assignment. They were chiefly counselors and critics of the kings in domestic affairs. As time went on and the nation went into spiritual decline, the prophetic office also degenerated (Micah 3:5–12). Then came a revival of the prophetic movement. With the ninth century B.C. the activity of the prophets entered a new phase. The work of the prophets became more comprehensive; they set down their prophecies in written form, and they extended their message to world affairs as they dealt with the national decline of Israel and the coming of the messianic kingdom. These years, from about 800 to about 450 B.C., were the years of the classical prophetic office in Old Testament history.

5. Consider the task and proclamation of an Old Testament prophet and compare these to Jesus and His ministry. In what ways was Jesus a "prophet"? In what ways did He differ?

6. To whom was the prophetic office given in Matthew 28:18–19? in 2 Timothy 2:2? in 2 Timothy 4:2? in 1 Peter 2:9? How do these passages apply to you? to your congregation?

7. In what way does the church today continue some of the tasks and functions of prophets? Who are the prophets today who speak for God?

Jesus, the greatest of all God's prophets, still speaks to us today through His Word and His church. Though many people seek new or personal revelations from Christ, the Scriptures given to us by Jesus provide all we need to know for our faith and Christian life. In the absolution of your pastor, the forgiveness of a friend, and the encouragement of fellow believers, hear the living and prophetic voice of the Savior, and pray confidently for His return, when you will see Him face-to-face.

In Closing

Encourage participants to begin the following activities:
- Begin reading the Books of Jeremiah and Lamentations.
- Mark passages considered outstanding. (These are to be reviewed in the final lesson of the course.)
- List passages that call for explanation. Many of them will be treated during the course. The rest should be submitted to the leader during Lesson 9.
- Read 2 Kings 22–25 and 2 Chronicles 34–36 to prepare for the next lesson.

Close with prayer.

Lesson 2

The World of Jeremiah

God called Jeremiah to do the best possible thing at the worst possible time. He performed his ministry in an age when the people of God as well as the other nations of the world were passing through one tragic crisis after another.

The Kingdom of Israel

At one time the 12 tribes of Israel had been a great nation, united under Saul, David, and Solomon.

8. Read 1 Kings 11:43–12:20. What important event is described? How would the event affect the nation and the future of the nation? What effect might it have on the religion of the people?

View a map of the nations of the Middle East after the reign of Solomon (see p. 109). Note the location and size of Judah and Israel compared to the surrounding nations.

Empires Crumble

The political and spiritual history of both Israel and Judah now went into a steady decline, with only brief periods of remission. Israel was the first to collapse, the final defeat coming in 722 B.C. at the hand of the Assyrians.

9. What caused the collapse of Israel, the Northern Kingdom? See 2 Kings 17:7–19.

Judah survived, but led a precarious existence as a petty nation constantly in danger of sharing Israel's fate of extinction. Egypt, located to the south, engaged in a struggle for world supremacy with nations to the east, Assyria, and later, Babylonia. The end of the kingdom of Judah, caught between these world powers, finally came in 586 B.C. The Babylonians conquered Jerusalem and destroyed the temple. Then they deported the people of Judah into foreign captivity (2 Kings 22–25; 2 Chronicles 34–36).

Before that final event Judah made one futile effort after another to escape destruction. When Assyria tried to become a world empire, Israel and other small kingdoms allied to resist Assyria. Judah refused to join the coalition. When these allied powers tried to force Judah to join them, Judah's kings looked to Assyria for help and became an Assyrian vassal. Later, when Assyria seemed to falter and Egypt was on the rise, the king of Judah joined in a rebellion against Assyria. But that rebellion failed and Judah returned to its former role as a puppet nation.

Then Assyria conquered Egypt. But the new Assyrian empire could not survive its internal problems or the rising opposition of other nations. Egypt seceded, the Arab tribes overran part of the empire, the Babylonians and Medes made a bid for supremacy, the Assyrian empire collapsed, and Judah became independent again. What a political tug-of-war!

10. Reflect on the situation in ancient Israel and the rise and fall of nations today. Briefly note similarities and differences without getting diverted into a political discussion.

Independence for Judah was only temporary. Babylonia and Egypt now fought one another for world control. Judah resisted Egypt, was conquered, and again became a vassal state, this time of Egypt. Once more the tide of power turned. Babylonia defeated Egypt, and Judah again belonged to Babylonia. When Judah later rebelled, Babylonia came to punish them. Nebuchadnezzar conquered Jerusalem and carried off the temple treasures and many thousands of the people, yet allowed the nation to continue.

18

11. What lesson(s) of history should Judah have learned from these circumstances? What spiritual lesson does the Lord invite Judah to learn in Jeremiah 1:16?

Through righteous kings such as Asa, Jehoshaphat, Hezekiah, and Josiah, God blessed the people of Judah. Through faithful prophets such as Isaiah and Jeremiah, He extended His grace and blessings. Despite the many changes in the nations, God and His Word did not change. They remain as steadfast and reliable today as they did for God's servants then.

12. Read Hebrews 13:7–8. What encouragement and hope does the passage provide for you and your congregation?

Judah had still not learned its lesson. It now listened to the voices of other small neighboring countries and again revolted. The Babylonian forces returned and this time completed the destruction of Judah (586 B.C.). Only poor peasants were allowed to remain, and Nebuchadnezzar appointed Gedaliah as the governor. When a revolt overthrew his government, his few remaining followers fled to Egypt and took with them Jeremiah, who through all these crises had remained in Judah. The Babylonian forces came to Judah for the third time, carried away more of its people, and for the next 40 years—until the exiled people were allowed to return home by the new world power of Persia—the kingdom of Judah no longer existed.

13. Why were the attempts of Judah to remain independent so futile? Refer again to 2 Kings 17:7–19. How could the kingdom of Judah have been preserved?

Jeremiah's Burden

14. Jeremiah prophesied under the last five kings of Judah and under the governor Gedaliah. You can read and summarize the work of these kings as follows:

Josiah: 640–609, 2 Kings 22:1–23:30

Jehoahaz: 609, 2 Kings 23:31–35

Jehoiakim: 609–598, 2 Kings 23:36–24:7

Jehoiachin: 598–597, 2 Kings 24:8–17

Zedekiah: 597–586, 2 Kings 24:18–25:21

The times of Jeremiah were times of political confusion, international conflict, and national disaster. When we add to this the tragic religious and social conditions within Judah, to be examined in later lessons, we begin to understand the burdens under which Jeremiah labored for 40 years of his life.

15. What similarities do you see between Middle East events in the time of Jeremiah and the political scene in that part of the world during recent years?

16. How would you describe the way in which religious opinions and movements affect the history of nations? Does religion change history or history change religion? Can you give illustrations?

17. Would it have been more difficult to be a child of God at Jeremiah's time—or now? Why?

Amid the chaotic, religious, and political events in ancient Judah, God sustained those who trusted in Him and followed His prophets. Consider how many great nations, leaders, and movements have disappeared or collapsed since Jeremiah's time. In contrast, consider how God has preserved His truth and the promise of forgiveness and salvation amid all this chaos and change! Through lonely prophets and faithful people like Jeremiah, God's blessings have continued and reached your ears this day.

When modern events discourage you, when you feel like you're the only person at your job or in your family who wants to walk in God's ways, remember how God sustained and comforted the faithful in Judah. In particular, rejoice that He sent for them His only Son, Jesus the Savior. For your sins and for your salvation, Jesus died alone on the cross. He suffered alone so that you might never be alone. He abides forever and will sustain you.

In Closing

Encourage participants to begin the following activities:
- As you watch the news this coming week, look for parallels between the events of Jeremiah's day and events today.
- Pray for your nation, your church, and your leaders.
- Read Jeremiah 1:1–3; 16:1–9; 25–29; and 34–44 to prepare for the next lesson.

Close with prayer.

Lesson 3

The Life and Character of Jeremiah

The Bible offers a wealth of information about the life of Jeremiah, but it does not give us his biography. We can reconstruct only a sketch of the principal events in his great career.

Jeremiah was a very young man when God made him a prophet in the year 626 B.C. (1:2, 6). He was born in Anathoth, a small village in Benjamin near Jerusalem, sometime between 650–645. His father was a priest (probably not the high priest of the same name under Josiah, 2 Kings 22), a descendant of Abiathar, who was exiled to Anathoth by Solomon (1 Kings 2:26–27). That would make Jeremiah a descendant of Eli (1 Samuel 1:3; 2:12–36) and, tradition says, of the family of Moses.

We are told nothing of Jeremiah's childhood and youth, but the words of his appointment by God suggest an early familiarity with religious matters (1:5). He was never married (16:1–2). Most of his ministry was spent in Jerusalem, where for 40 years he fulfilled his office until the destruction of the city in 586. Then he was active in Mizpah (40:1–6) until Judeans fleeing to Egypt in 582 took him with them to Tahpanhes (42:1–43:7). There he continued to preach (43:8–44:30). An apocryphal book from the first century A.D., *The Lives of the Prophets,* reports that his own countrymen stoned him to death.

18. Discuss the struggles of Jeremiah. How do his struggles compare with the struggles faced by those who speak for God today?

Controversy

Throughout his long ministry, Jeremiah was often the center of controversy. Although a prophet, he also lived a martyr's life. The early church father Origen has been attributed as saying that Jeremiah "was long a martyr before he actually became a martyr."

19. Tell how the following passages illustrate the truth of the above statements: 1:18–19; 11:21–23; 12:6; 15:10; 20:1–7; 26:20–24; 36:5; 36:26; 38:6–13

Jeremiah's Task

The life and work of Jeremiah begins in the middle of the era of classical prophecy in Israel. His task is particularly difficult, for the scope of his ministry extends far beyond the land of Judah, and his message will have world-shaking effects. It will destroy and restore entire nations (1:10). He is to be the mouthpiece of the Lord to the whole world of his time, with the full authority of God resting upon him. It is small wonder that Jeremiah is reluctant to accept the appointment and pleads his own incompetence (1:6). But he must remember that God made him for His work (1:5), that God's Word has come to him and rests upon his lips (1:2, 4, 9, 13), and that he can depend on the full support of God for his mission (1:7, 12, 17–19).

20. Jeremiah receives two visions (1:11–12 and 1:13–19). What significance do you see in the branch of the almond tree (1:11)? in the boiling pot (1:13)? In what way do you think the first vision (1:11–12) gave Jeremiah the courage to accept God's call?

Jeremiah has a unique assignment. While his colleagues before him were like physicians attending a seriously ill patient, Jeremiah became the one to call the condition irreversible and to pronounce the patient dead. His was the task of declaring to an impenitent and stubborn people that the time of judgment had come and that their destruction was close at hand. Jeremiah preaches doom, yet there remains a small light of hope (1:10), for death and destruction will be followed by life and reconstruction. This theme was repeated in a positive way in the New Testament, where, through Jesus, death and destruction is followed by eternal life and reconstruction (see 1 Corinthians 15:20–26).

21. Read Exodus 3:7–22; Judges 6:1–16; and Isaiah 6:1–13. What similarities to Jeremiah 1 do you see? What assurance does each person receive? What do the events say about our "call"?

22. Was the persecution Jeremiah suffered unique? Name some other examples from biblical or later history of God's people. Check Hebrews 11:32–40 for biblical examples.

23. Why can we expect the same kind of treatment that Jeremiah and God's other prophets received? Read John 16:1–4; 15:18–20; and 1 John 3:13. What might it mean if Christians are not hated or persecuted?

24. After the American Revolutionary War, the Roman Catholic Church in the new country's frontier was in need of priests. An appeal was made in France to enlist the French clergy. It included this statement: "We offer you No Salary; No Recompense; No Holidays; Few Consolations; Many Disappointments; Frequent Sickness; a Violent or Lonely Death; an Unknown Grave." Many French priests responded to this call. How far would such recruitment efforts go today? Would the church of today be justified in making such an appeal?

When Michelangelo painted the figure of Jeremiah on the ceiling of the Sistine Chapel, he portrayed him as a man of great strength bowed under a great burden. Above each of the prophet's shoulders the painter placed a different character. Over one shoulder appears a daughter of Zion in despair. Over the other shoulder stands a son of Judah looking into the distance, a symbol of hope.

25. Describe some situations when Christians still are faced with heavy burdens. How can they endure these crosses? What encouragement can they receive from the example of Jeremiah? from the Gospel?

The Weeping Prophet

26. Read Lamentations 3:1–21. List terms or phrases that express the prophet's sorrow.

"Jeremiah is generally called the Weeping Prophet. That name creates the impression that he was an effeminate person, lacking manly strength of character, lamenting in season and out of season, like the mourning women of Israel always ready to shed tears on the slightest occasion. It is true that Jeremiah was of a warmhearted, sympathetic nature. He did shed tears when he saw the ever-increasing wickedness and stubborn self-hardening of his people, whose salvation he so fervently desired, or when he realized that the horrible judgments of the just God were drawing ever closer and finally saw them poured out like a devastating flood on people and country. Yet by the grace of God he became a tower of strength, a real man's man, one of God's outstanding heroes. Not once did he break down in public. Facing his people, he was invariably the man of God, the messenger of the Lord's mercy, calling to repentance the nation he loved with a love as tender as that of a mother, as sincere as that of a faithful friend, sticking closer than a brother. His love of his people, however, did not interfere with his sense of duty, his love and obedience toward God. Unsparingly he

26

pronounced God's judgments upon the impenitent without respect of persons. Like walls of brass he stood firm against frenzied prophets, fanatic priests, frantic people, furious kings. Calmly he faced this pack of snarling wolves ready to murder him. Neither defamation, nor persecution, nor imprisonment, nor threats of death kept him from speaking whatever God commanded him. Only when alone with himself and his God did he give voice to his agonized feelings, his doubts and fears, his heartaches and gnawing grief, his bitterness and his maledictions. And from every battle he rose more than a conqueror by the grace and power of Him who was the LORD, his Strength, his Fortress, and his Refuge in the day of affliction, because this LORD was Jehovah, his Righteousness" (Theodore Laetsch, *Jeremiah,* Concordia Classic Commentary Series [St. Louis: Concordia Publishing House, 1952], xi–xii).

27. In what way was Jeremiah a living example of John 16:33 and Acts 14:22?

In Closing

Encourage participants to do the following activities:
- Close by reading in unison Lamentations 3:19–33.
- Sing "Great Is Thy Faithfulness" (based on Lamentations 3:22–23).
- Look for an opportunity this week to console someone who is struggling.
- Read Jeremiah 3–6 to prepare for the next lesson.

Close with prayer.

Lesson 4

Early Prophecies

Jeremiah's homeland was a tiny kingdom surrounded by powerful empires that finally overwhelmed it. Jeremiah mourns the calamity in eloquent words (4:19–31). But the real tragedy is not the demise of a nation—it is the theological and spiritual death of a people turned faithless and idolatrous. "The same Lord who saw the wickedness of Israel, His people, and because of this wickedness destroyed the city of Shiloh (v. 14), the sanctuary (v. 12), and about a century before Jeremiah the whole seed of Ephraim (v. 15), sees also Judah's works equaling Israel's wickedness and surpassing it (v. 13; also 3:11) in spite of the oft-repeated and eager pleas of the Lord (v. 13). He is now ready to cast all of Judah out of His sight as He cast out all the seed of Ephraim" (Laetsch, p. 96.)

An Early Sermon

An example of Jeremiah's early sermons is found in 2:1–3:5. Note the richness of the imagery, the directness of the message, the vehemence of the language.

28. Which verses or expressions in this section do you find particularly forceful?

29. Is there a connection between this preaching of Jeremiah and the events of King Josiah's reform (2 Kings 22:1–23:25)?

The Gospel Prevails

Read 3:11–18. The preaching of the Law can never stand alone. Jeremiah must speak God's message of grace and promise as well.

30. What does the manner of Jeremiah's preaching say to the church of today?

31. What is the Gospel? What does it say to you? What does it mean for you? for your congregation?

32. Why is it never enough simply to condemn sin or to denounce immorality? What is the purpose of "laying down the law"?

Dishonesty

Read 5:23–29. Where there is no knowledge of God, one would expect to find greed, treachery, and social injustice—open rejection of any objective principles of right and wrong. But when God finds this among those whom He calls "My people," then His judgment must certainly follow.

Here the charge is that the people of Judah have made personal wealth and advantage the goals of their lives (v. 28). They seek profit and gain by any means, with no concern for the welfare of others, even at the expense of the fatherless and the needy—those least able to defend themselves. The household of God has become a jungle governed by "the survival of the fittest." The children of God have rejected their Father, and now they turn on one another.

Such conduct violates a basic principle of the will of God in the second table of the Law (Commandments 4–10). This is, of course, the way of the world. It is also a clear demonstration of the self-centered life as a basic trait of fallen mankind. But God's people should be above that. Their position of privilege puts them under greater responsibility. (See Luke 12:47–48 and Matthew 11:20–24.)

33. How would modern business practices fare if examined on the basis of 5:23–29? What seems to be the principle of decision making today?

34. How does the present-day climate of selfish materialism enter into the life of many Christian people? In what way does the stress on "things" and "profit" make your Christian life difficult?

A Nation in Love with Sin

Read 5:30–31. This charge covers the entire nation: prophets, priests, and people. The prophets have failed in their task of proclaiming the Word of the Lord (recall Lesson 1). The priests have acted like puppets of popular opinion as they have conducted their worship services. And the people are no less guilty—they have loved the lies (see 2 Timothy 4:3). Thus the Lord's accusation of faithlessness is directed against all—none is guiltless. The nation has rejected the Lord.

35. Who, then, was to blame for the faithlessness of Judah and its downfall?

36. To what extent are such people responsible for errors in teaching and practice today? Is it any different today?

Our Lord and His apostles clearly taught that faith alone saves, not obedience to the Commandments. Yet He said that He had not come to destroy the Law, and the apostles consistently urge Christians to observe the will of God in their life and to be different from the world of unbelief about them. There is a difference between liberty and license, and between a life under the Law and a life within the Law. And it takes wisdom to know the difference.

Praise God for the wisdom we receive in His Son, Jesus Christ! "For the foolishness of God is wiser than man's wisdom, and the weakness of God is stronger than man's strength" (1 Corinthians 1:25). In Christ we are wise not only for this life and age but, more important, we are wise for the life and ages to come.

In Closing

Encourage participants to begin the following activities:

- Read Jeremiah 7–10 to prepare for the next lesson.
- List names of leaders in the government, the church, and other institutions for whom you will pray throughout the week.

Close with prayer.

Lesson 5

The Temple Message

Relationships deteriorate and people grow distant from one another in direct proportion to the deterioration of their relationship to God and their distance from Him. God's Old Testament people showed the truth of this equation often (e.g., Amos 2:4–8). It was especially evident in the time of Jeremiah.

The Temple Sermon

In 7:1–15 we find what is known as Jeremiah's temple sermon. While there is no clear statement here regarding its date, it probably belongs to the time when the Book of the Law had been rediscovered under King Josiah and the contents of the covenant published.

37. What does this sermon say about the real effectiveness of Josiah's reform?

38. What basic problem does Jeremiah address?

39. How does the message relate to our religious life today?

Oppression

Focus on 7:5–10. Here sins against the neighbor and against society are mentioned first. This follows the line of thought in 1 John 3:17 and 4:20. Add to this the fact that the world judges the sincerity of the Christian and the value of the Christian Gospel by the visible evidence of that Gospel in the day-to-day life of the Christian, and the importance of these words in Jeremiah for us is clear.

40. What would Jeremiah's message in 7:5–10 say to us today?

41. Does the gradual development of the welfare state have any bearing on our observance of the "second great commandment" (Matthew 22:39)?

My House—A Den of Robbers?

Read Jeremiah 7:11 and Matthew 21:12–16. Jeremiah's temple sermon pointedly accuses God's people of living a lie in their pretense at worship. His words become the text for the later temple sermon of our Lord, a sermon of action rather than one of many words, in which Jesus pronounces judgment on the hypocrisy of that time.

42. What do the above passages say about God's response to abuses of worship? about the true purpose of worship?

43. What kind of "temple sermon" would Jeremiah or Jesus preach in our church next Sunday?

Gross Idolatry

Read 7:16–20. Here is the evidence in support of God's charge of faithlessness. Look at the daily life of the people, when they are not engaged in the formal worship of God. You can't tell the difference between them and the heathen! While they claim devotion to God (7:4, 10), their worship is pure formality, lip service and not life service. Once God laid upon the homes of His people the responsibility of teaching and promoting the honor of His name (Deuteronomy 6:6–9), but that has all been forgotten. Here parents and children now spend their time and energy not in the service of the Lord, but in the pursuit of what they find more pleasurable and meaningful, the worship of the sensuous and of the material, here represented by the "Queen of Heaven."

Now read Jeremiah 44:1–10. This is perhaps 25 years later. The sins of their lip service now bring their reward. God has warned and God has acted. Jerusalem has fallen, and most of the people have been taken to Babylon. But these people who have fled to Egypt remain as stubborn as before. They persist in their rejection of God and in their worship of the Queen of Heaven, and even rationalize and defend their wickedness (44:17–19). For this they, too, shall perish when Egypt falls under the judgment of the Lord.

44. How do lives today reflect the pattern of Judah in these two passages?

45. Is it realistic to expect God's people to be different from others? See Romans 12:1–2.

46. What kinds of pressures both from self and others are put upon people who try to "live" their faith? What tensions can this create for the contemporary Christian?

God's Questions

We frequently have questions for God. In times of doubt or disappointment, we wonder whether God is hearing us or whether He cares. In Bible class or catechism class, we may question what God teaches and even press our church leaders for answers.

For the ancient Israelites, oral questions and answers formed the basic teaching method. Students would gather around their teacher to recite basic texts and answer their teacher's questions about them. A student who had learned the lesson would also have the opportunity to question the teacher (e.g., Luke 2:46–50).

However, in Jeremiah 8 God is the One who has questions. Through Jeremiah He questions the people of Jerusalem, especially the scribes and wise men who would gather at the gate of the city or the temple for discussion. In other words, God is testing the faith of those who claim to be teachers in Judah during the reign of Jehoiakim or Josiah.

Read the following questions and call on the background information about Jeremiah's situation, which you studied in the first lessons. Then discuss the application of these questions for today.

47. "When men fall down, do they not get up? When a man turns away, does he not return? Why then have these people turned away? Why does Jerusalem always turn away?" (Jeremiah 8:4–5a). Read Jeremiah 8:5b–6 and 15:6 to form your answers.

48. Discuss how your congregation handles cases of unrepentance or members who do not return for worship. Is there a limit to pleas for repentance or calls inviting people to return to worship? Read 1 Corinthians 5:9–12 and Matthew 18:15–18.

49. "How can you say, 'We are wise, for we have the law of the LORD,' when actually the lying pen of the scribes has handled it falsely?" (Jeremiah 8:8). Read Jeremiah 8:7. What event during

Josiah's reign revealed the unfaithfulness of the scribes? (See 2 Kings 22:8–13 for help.)

50. How does your congregation make the reading and study of God's Word a priority for your members? for your community?

51. "Since they [the scribes] have rejected the word of the LORD, what kind of wisdom do they have?" (Jeremiah 8:9b). Read 1 Kings 4:29–34 and 2 Kings 17:32–34.

52. "Are they [the leaders] ashamed of their loathsome conduct?" (Jeremiah 8:12a). Read Jeremiah 8:12b and 13:25–27.

53. Is shame an effective way to foster good behavior? Why or why not?

54. "Listen to the cry of My people from a land far away: 'Is the LORD not in Zion? Is her King no longer there?' " (Jeremiah 8:19a). Read Jeremiah 30:23–31:2 to answer these questions of God's people.

55. Are there times in your life when God seems absent? How can faith and hope survive in such times? Read Lamentations 5:19–22.

56. Jeremiah wonders, "Is there no balm in Gilead? Is there no physician there? Why then is there no healing for the wound of my people?" (Jeremiah 8:21–22). Read Deuteronomy 32:39; Jeremiah 30:17 and 33:6 to form your answer to Jeremiah's questions.

My Glory: I Know God

Read 9:23–24. Wisdom, might, and riches as the objects of human desire and worship—there is nothing new under the sun! These are good gifts of God and useful in His service, but they can become substitutes for God. Displacement of God was the problem already in Paradise (Genesis 3:1–6), and it remains a threat to faith today. But cultural, material, and technical advantages are not at the top of God's scale of values. They ultimately fail (Ecclesiastes 1), as people have always learned by tragic experience, and as humanity still discovers. One thing alone abides, and that is faith in God and His constant grace and mercy. It is true for the individual as well as for the nation, for the people of Jeremiah's day and for our own today.

57. What are the most desired goals of our time: wisdom, might, riches, or faith? Which do you choose?

58. How do we determine greatness among us, perhaps even in the church?

59. A great issue for people in Jeremiah's day was national security. The work of the priests and the false prophets would have focused on this issue. On what basis do we evaluate national security today? Read Psalm 33:16–17; 118:8–9; and 127:1–2. Also read Nehemiah 4:16–23.

60. What does Jesus teach about "knowing" God (John 17:3)? What does it really mean to know God?

Idols: Like Scarecrows?

Read 10:1–16. The thought of the previous section is here extended and refined in a classic contrast between all man-made idols and the everlasting God. Note the prophet's cutting sarcasm and biting irony against false gods, and his adoring worship of the one true God. Those poor, defenseless, ridiculous idols—that great, living, incomparable God! Here are words to rebuke our unbelief, to shame our anxiousness, to strengthen our faith, to challenge our commitment. Perhaps read the story of Elijah and the prophets of Baal (1 Kings 18:20–40).

61. Analyze Jeremiah 10:1–16 under the two column headings below. List the points of Jeremiah in contrasting pairs. What then is the bottom line?

Idols   Lord

62. In view of this, how do you then account for human unbelief?

In Jeremiah 9:23 we read that we cannot boast in our wisdom, strength, or riches. However, in 10:12, 16 Jeremiah does just that! He boasts in the Lord as his power, wisdom, understanding, and portion/inheritance. By *knowing* the Lord and trusting in Him we gain this right to boast in our blessings. Jeremiah's boast anticipates the boasting of the apostle Paul, who wrote, "We demolish arguments and every pretension that sets itself up against the knowledge of God, and we take captive every thought to make it obedient to Christ. But, 'Let him who boasts boast in the Lord.' For it is not the one who commends himself who is approved, but the one whom the Lord commends" (2 Corinthians 10:5, 17–18).

In Closing

Encourage participants to begin the following activities:
- Read Jeremiah 11–20.
- List reasons you have for boasting in the Lord.
- Speak of God's blessing to you with a member of your family, a friend, or a neighbor.

Close with prayer.

Lesson 6

The Covenant and the Potter's Wheel

Judah Fails a History Lesson

Read 11:1–17. God's people have broken the covenant of God (v. 10). The reference is to the time of the Exodus, when at Mount Sinai the Lord established a covenant with His people in which they agreed to serve Him (Exodus 19:3–8). But Israel had not kept its word in the days of Moses (Exodus 32; Numbers 14).

Now under the reform movement of Josiah the people have responded to the reading of the rediscovered Book of the Law and have renewed their ancient promise (2 Kings 23:1–3). But again the nation is faithless, and the reform is only an outward sham. Each city honors its own god, and Jerusalem is filled with altars dedicated to Baal. Disaster looms. Idols cannot save the people from the impending destruction, and the Lord will not help in their impenitent state. Not even the intercession of Jeremiah will be of any value. The treachery of an unfaithful people is the source of Judah's destruction.

63. How can subtle idolatry slip into the life of an individual or a church?

64. What are some of today's "other gods"?

65. How can confusion about who and what is most important lead to faithlessness among the people of God?

They Will Be My People

Compare Jeremiah 32:37–41 with 2 Corinthians 6:16. Paul's quotation from Jeremiah indicates not only his own familiarity with the prophet, but also that the words of Jeremiah were highly regarded as God's own Word, to be used with authority for the strengthening of the New Testament faith and as exhortation to God's people of all the ages.

66. What comfort do these words have for you personally?

The Potter's Wheel

Read 18:1–10. The sight of a potter plying his or her craft was common in Judah. Isaiah uses this imagery (30:14 and 64:8), and so does Paul (Romans 9:19–24). God is the Potter—patient, persevering, and in full control. Mankind is the clay—formless, passive, and without value apart from the Potter's work. The message of Jeremiah is twofold. God will shape His people if they repent, but He will destroy and discard them if they remain impenitent.

67. Read Jeremiah 19:1–2, 10–12; 2 Timothy 2:20–21; and 2 Corinthians 4:7. What does the parable of the potter say in each instance?

68. How does faith respond to the lessons in the parable of the potter?

A Time of Depression

Even great people of God have times of depression. Jeremiah 20:7–18 reflects the intense struggle within the prophet as he recalls the promises of God and then compares them with the painful realities of his personal experience. Here, too, is an example of the strategy of Satan, who attacks the child of God and seeks out vulnerable spots to destroy him or her.

69. What wish does Jeremiah actually express here? Can you name similar instances of despair in Scripture? (See 1 Kings 19:1–8 and Job 3.)

70. Is Jeremiah's wish sinful? How might the words "Thy will be done" and the parable of the potter address Jeremiah's thoughts? Read Philippians 1:23–26.

71. Where does Jeremiah finally find help with his deep depression? Read 1:19.

72. Is it possible that pastors and Christian teachers still share the inner tensions and conflicts of Jeremiah? What could cause this? How can we help prevent it? How can we help our pastors in times of discouragement?

A Time of Hope

Read 23:1–8. There is a balm in Gilead (8:22). There is a light and hope for the people of God. Think of this passage in terms of its messianic promise and its fulfillment in the New Testament. When the great Son of David, the Lord Jesus Christ, comes to make His perfect righteousness available to the world, the people of God—out of all the nations under heaven—shall dwell in perfect safety under His rule and at the last enter their eternal homeland.

73. How do these words give you comfort and hope? In what way do they personally reach you?

In Closing

Encourage participants to begin the following activities:
- Read Jeremiah 25–29.
- Identify someone you know who struggles with depression or worry and offer encouragement from God's Word through a phone call, card, or conversation.

Close with prayer.

Lesson 7

The Exile

A Word from Jeremiah

In the first conquest of Jerusalem, Nebuchadnezzar had deported perhaps as many as 17,000 of the skilled class of people to Babylonia. There they were granted considerable freedom, including freedom of worship. They had prophets such as Ezekiel and Daniel. Some of the captives held responsible positions in government (see Daniel 1:3–7). There was communication with the homeland (Jeremiah 29:1, 25). Not all of the people later returned home; many prospered in Babylon and chose to remain in that land (Ezra 1:2–6).

But for the most part the people suffered deeply under their separation from their holy city and country (see Psalm 137). They refused to accept their fate. They looked for an early return home, and false prophets agitated among them to build up false hopes of a short captivity (Jeremiah 28:1–17; 29:8–9). The people were restless and unhappy. They needed positive encouragement and practical advice. They got this from Jeremiah by letter from Jerusalem.

Even though God had sent them into exile, He was still in control of the situation as the God of Israel (29:4), although His people were strangers in a strange land. They were to remain faithful to Him and trust Him and depend on Him to keep His promise of a return home in His own good time. In the meantime, they were to be realistic in their adjustment to their new situation.

74. What kind of lifestyle were they to lead in Babylon (29:5–6)?

75. What does Jeremiah ask of the captives in verse 7? What would your reaction be to such a request?

A Word for Today

Here is a message for the people of God in every age. We know that we are "aliens and strangers on earth" and that "here we do not have an enduring city, but we are looking for the city that is to come" (Hebrews 11:8–16; 13:14). We are warned against losing our identity as the people of God (Romans 12:1–2). But we are in the world and as long as we are here, we are to meet our responsibilities.

76. What does Matthew 5:13–16 tell us about the nature of these responsibilities?

Christians must be concerned for the social, political, and economic welfare of their human community, even in—especially in— times of turbulence and disorder. In this connection, study Paul's words to Titus (Titus 1:5, 12; 3:1–2).

77. How was Titus to react to this unhappy situation? What does this say about our response to the Gospel?

78. As a stranger and exile in this life, are you living up to the words of Jeremiah 29:5–7 now? If you were on trial for being Christian, would there be enough evidence to convict you?

79. What encouragement in word and example in Christian living can we expect from our spiritual leaders?

80. Discuss the involvement of Christians in community affairs as instruments of God, who bring His blessings to the surrounding people.

81. What are the opportunities within our immediate reach?

82. Can you cite instances where the promise of 29:7 was fulfilled?

83. How can God's people survive and even prosper under hostile rulers without compromising their faith?

84. Read Matthew 5:44–48. How does this teaching test the genuineness of our commitment to our Lord and our trust in Him? (Note also 1 Timothy 2:1–4.)

85. Read Jeremiah 29:10–14. List the promises God makes to the people through Jeremiah.

86. As a group read aloud 29:11–13. In place of the word *you,* state your name or the name of your congregation. How does this help you appreciate the promise of this passage?

In Closing

Encourage participants to begin the following activities:
- Draw up personal plans for the future.
- Assess your plans in view of God's Word and pray for His blessing.
- Read Jeremiah 30–33.

Close with prayer.

Lesson 8

The Book of Comfort

If Jeremiah was a prophet of doom and disaster, he was equally a messenger of hope and promise. In other words, he clearly presented both aspects of the nature of God as revealed to Moses on Mount Sinai (Exodus 34:6–7). This is nowhere more clearly seen than in what is known as the "Book of Comfort," Jeremiah 30–33.

The Promise of Restoration

Jeremiah promised that both Judah and Israel would return from exile and rebuild their cities and palaces, while their oppressors would be destroyed (30:3–11, 18–24). It is not as though the people deserved to survive. By their wickedness they had been the cause of their own disaster, and God's pronouncements of just punishment had to stand (30:12–16). In spite of their sin, out of His pure grace and mercy, God healed their incurable wound (30:17).

87. Read Isaiah 61:2–6 for imagery similar to Jeremiah 30:17. Can you recall other passages in Scripture that picture God as the Great Healer?

88. What is the real meaning of *grace*? See Romans 11:5–6 and Ephesians 2:8–9.

The Promise of Everlasting Love

Note the repetition of the promise and the renewal of God's blessings in 31:2–6. As once He loved His people, so He continues to love them, despite their disobedience. Even His chastisements are not intended to destroy them but to draw them closer to Himself. (See Hebrews 12:5–11.) In mercy God promises a new covenant, new in its fulfillment in Christ, to whom the Old Testament points; new to the people of God, who will know Him in faith and manifest their faith by keeping the Law in their hearts and acting according to it (31:31–34).

89. How does 31:28 reflect the call of Jeremiah in 1:10?

90. What does 31:28 say about the task of the church today (see Ephesians 4:15)?

91. Does God punish the sins of penitent believers? Will He make their sins public on Judgment Day? (See 31:34; Isaiah 38:17; Micah 7:19.)

Rachel Weeping for Her Children

Compare Jeremiah 31:15 with Matthew 2:17–18. Rachel, the favorite wife of Jacob, died at the birth of her son Benjamin and was buried near Bethlehem (Genesis 35:16–20).

92. How do Jeremiah and Matthew bring this fact to mind? How do we know that Jeremiah 31:15 is a messianic prophecy? Read Jeremiah 31:16–17. What hope does God hold up to the Israelites as they walk past the grave of Rachel into exile? What even greater hope lies in the future for Israel?

A New Covenant

Read Jeremiah 31:31–34 and Hebrews 8:8–12; 10:16–17. This is the longest direct quotation from Jeremiah in the New Testament and clearly indicates the importance of the prophet and his message for the church to the end of time.

93. Contrast the old and new covenants.

94. What accusation about the sincerity of Christians do people often make? What is the justification for the accusation? How would you respond to it?

95. Why would the Letter to the Hebrews support its Gospel message with a quotation from Jeremiah?

96. Our Lord and His apostles often quoted from Jeremiah. What would this fact lead us to believe about the book? What value does Jeremiah have for us? How does it point to Christ?

The Promise of Answered Prayer

The real-estate transaction in 32:1–15 provides the setting for what follows. It is symbolic of God's promise to restore Judah (v. 15). But Jeremiah has some misgivings. In his prayer he praises the past mercies of God and confesses the sins of the people, and then he asks how such a restoration could be possible. The fact that, in the face of great wickedness, God could still show even greater goodness is beyond his understanding. God's response is that the deserved judgment will happen (26–35), but that in His mercy He will not hold the sins of His own children against them forever but will forgive them and restore their fortune (36–44).

97. How does the story of Judah illustrate what Paul says in Ephesians 3:20?

98. Can you supply other instances where God restored His people in the face of desperate situations?

The Promise of Future Glory

Jeremiah 33:1–13 restates and emphasizes the previous promises of restoration (32:37–44). But now this vision expands, and Judah becomes the prophetic symbol of the people of God to the end of time. It represents the New Testament church of the Messiah, the Christ, the descendant of King David (33:15). It is His name, "The LORD Our Righteousness," that is laid upon the church (v. 16), for in Him alone the church becomes acceptable to God, and the church alone proclaims the Gospel of His righteousness (see 1 Peter 2:4–10 and Romans 4:16–17). That new covenant of God remains unshakably certain (Jeremiah 33:20–21, 25–26).

99. Discuss this statement: "Outside of the church there is no salvation."

100. The hymn "The Church's One Foundation" states that "the Church shall never perish." (See *The Lutheran Hymnal* 473:3.) In which sense is this true? What does that mean for you?

Slavery

Read 34:8–22. See also Deuteronomy 15:1, 12–18. The periodic emancipation of slaves was once a social institution in Israel, but it had fallen into disuse by Jeremiah's time. When the land was under attack by the Babylonians, it was expedient to free the slaves, who would then not be a burden on their owners, but would be left to their own resources in a time of scarcity. Freed slaves might also be more inclined to serve the nation in battle. But when the danger was past or lessened because the siege of Jerusalem was relaxed (Jeremiah 37:1–10), the slaveholders reneged on their word and took back their slaves. In verse 17 God passes judgment on this behavior.

101. Today there is much emphasis on humanitarianism. How might Jeremiah's charge of opportunism apply to many humanitarian ventures today? Can you cite specific examples of abuse through humanitarian efforts?

102. Evaluate life principles such as these: "Hire the handicapped—it's good business"; "We must employ a quota of minority people to get government subsidy or to avoid legal action"; "Crime does not pay"; and "Honesty is the best policy." What is often the real and hidden reason behind "good" ethical decisions?

103. What is the responsibility of the church in matters of social welfare for those outside its own membership?

104. What is the message of the church regarding conditions of human oppression in the world today?

A Call to Repentance

Read Jeremiah 36. For 23 years Jeremiah has proclaimed his message of repentance and judgment. Not all of the people have listened; some have not heard him at all. Now in this critical year, when Babylon has become the ruling world power and the judgment over Judah is about to begin, God tells Jeremiah to put it all together in this dramatic call to repentance.

Baruch, Jeremiah's scribe or secretary, reads the scroll, first in the temple and then before the assembled princes. Now the king, who seems to have been on a holiday, must hear it. But there the words fall on hostile ears. Not only does King Jehoiakim show his personal contempt for the message by mutilating and burning the book, but he also orders the arrest of Baruch and Jeremiah for having produced it. The Lord overturns the king's decision by saving His servants and by replacing and enlarging the manuscript.

105. What does this event say about (a) the task of the church? (b) the reception given to the message of the Lord? (c) the Lord's concern for His Word and for His messengers? (d) the future of Christian preaching?

In Closing

Encourage participants to begin the following activities:
- Read Lamentations 3:40–50 responsively.
- Celebrate the blessings we have received in the new covenant.
- Read Jeremiah 46–51 and Lamentations 4–5.

Close with prayer.

Lesson 9

Lord of All the Nations

From the name of our prophet has come the noun *jeremiad*. Most often it means a weeping lament—an expression of grief. But the word also has the meaning of tirade—angry denunciation. The reason for the latter meaning may lie in chapters 25 and 46–51. The prophet insists that Judah must be scourged for her unfaithfulness to God, and the surrounding nations will serve as God's tool for the scourging (25:1–11). But even the instruments of punishment will be made to feel the wrath of God and will be rejected because they, in turn, likewise rejected God (25:12–38).

Twenty nations are marked for judgment by Jeremiah, of whom 10 are specifically named in chapters 46–51. Among them are nations that were the traditional enemies of Israel since the days of Moses and Joshua.

106. Consider some of the vivid descriptions of judgment listed in chapter 25. How might God's words of judgment remain the same today? How might they differ?

Lord of Egypt

Egypt is the first to be named in the series of judgments against the nations (46:1–2). It was Israel's first oppressor and resisted God in the days of the Exodus (Exodus 1–14). Egypt plundered Jerusalem after Solomon's death (1 Kings 14:25–26), allied itself with Assyria against God's people, and was instrumental in the fall of three kings of Judah (Jeremiah 46:1–2). Egypt suffers her promised (46:12) defeat in 605 B.C., when Nebuchadnezzar defeated Pharaoh Neco at Carchemish

55

on the Euphrates. Yet Egypt became a stronghold of the early Christian church.

107. How does 46:26b explain the changes in Egypt? What does this show about the nature of God? Read the earlier prophecy of Isaiah 19:19–25.

Lord of the Philistines

The Philistines had often harassed Israel in the past, in the days of the Judges and of kings Saul and David (e.g., Judges 14–15; 1 Samuel 13–14; 2 Samuel 5:17–25). They had seduced Israel to idolatry (Judges 10:6) and mocked God (1 Samuel 17). Now their cries, not of repentance, but of anguish, will go unheard.

108. Philistia must fall (ch. 47). How terrible will this destruction be?

Lord of Moab

Moab, another traditional enemy of Israel (Numbers 22–24), is next on the list to go down to destruction (ch. 48). But note here also a sign of future hope for the later descendants of Moab (48:47).

109. What is a possible reason for the mercy God would show to Moab? See Ruth 1:22 and Matthew 1:5.

Lord of Babylon

The fate of Ammon, Edom, Damascus, Kedar, Hazor, and Elam is prophesied in chapter 49. However, more than all of these, Babylon shall suffer the vengeance of the Lord. It becomes the subject of an extended prophecy (chs. 50–51). This nation had served as the last of the Lord's scourges for His people and had made the destruction of Judah and Jerusalem total. So it would likewise be totally destroyed (50:39–40), and "then heaven and earth and all that is in them will shout for joy over Babylon" (51:48).

110. What is the significance of the reference to "Babylon" in Revelation 14:8 and Revelation 17–18?

Lord of All

God remains the Lord, not over His people alone, but over all the earth. These chapters are a powerful witness to the eternal truth of Psalm 2:1–6 and to the great confidence of Psalm 46. They are a comfort for those who believe in God, a warning for those who defy Him, an invitation to trust in Him, and a promise of His grace and mercy (e.g., 46:26; 48:47; 49:6, 39).

111. What lesson might the world of today take from this portion of Jeremiah?

112. What is the message for God's people in the church, both as comfort and as warning?

113. How does this portion of Jeremiah help us understand Ephesians 1:20–23?

In Closing

Encourage participants to begin the following activities:

- Consider the progress of the Gospel among the nations listed by Jeremiah.
- Pray for a renewal of Christian faith and missions in these nations.
- Learn about current mission efforts in the Near East.

Close with prayer.

Lesson 10

Jeremiah and Jesus

When Jesus asked His disciples at Caesarea Philippi, "Who do people say the Son of Man is?" they said, "Some say . . . Jeremiah" (Matthew 16:13–14). That was not simply a flippant remark, but an opinion based on a considered judgment. The people of Christ's time knew Jeremiah's life and work of 600 years before. And as they observed the ministry of Jesus, they saw certain similarities between the two men, which suggested to them that a prophet like Jeremiah had been sent to them again.

Use the following questions to compare Jeremiah with Jesus.

114. What similarities existed between the world powers, Babylon and Rome?

115. How did the home communities of Jeremiah and Jesus receive them? See Jeremiah 11:21 and Luke 4:16–30.

116. At what age did each prophet show an awareness of the Father's call? See Jeremiah 1:4–7 and Luke 2:41–50.

117. What relationship did each prophet have with the religious leaders of the day? Review these passages: 1:18–19; 11:21–23; 12:6;

15:10; 20:1–7; 26:20–24; 36:5, 26; and 38:6–13. Compare these to events in Jesus' life recorded in Matthew 21 and 23.

Jewish people after the exile honored Jeremiah very highly. The ministry of Jesus reminded them of him.

118. How did each prophet regard the mere formalism and ritualism they saw in people's devotion? See Jeremiah 7:1–10 and Matthew 6:1–2, 16–18.

119. Compare the emotion and tone of Matthew 23:37–39 with portions of Lamentations. In what sense were both Jesus and Jeremiah "weeping" prophets?

120. What similarities do you see in the sufferings of Jeremiah and Jesus?

A Great Difference

Jeremiah and Jesus were, however, also very different.

121. What differences do you find when you compare Jeremiah 12:1–3 and 18:23 with Luke 23:34? What other differences can you list?

122. In what ways can Jeremiah and Jesus serve as models for your life?

123. Would you consider it an honor to be compared to Jeremiah? Why or why not?

124. When people look at us, in what ways do they find reason to think of us as "little Christs"?

In Closing

Encourage participants to begin the following activities:
- Read Jeremiah 31:31–34 as preparation for receiving the Lord's Supper.
- Pray for the complete fullness of God's promise in Jeremiah 31:34.

Close with prayer.

Lesson 11

A Summary of the Message

In his preface to the Book of Jeremiah, Martin Luther offers these thoughts as a summary:

"To understand the prophet Jeremiah, one does not need a great deal of commentary if one only examines the historical record of the kings under whom he prophesied. For his sermons reflect the national situation of his time.

"In the first place, the country was filled with vice and idolatry. The people killed the prophets and wanted vice and idolatry to go unchecked. Therefore the first part, to Chapter 20, is almost purely a rebuke and complaint about the wickedness of the Jews.

"Second, he foretells also the impending punishment, the destruction of Jerusalem, in fact also the punishment of all the heathen nations. And yet he offers comfort, and promises that at a definite and determined time, after the punishment is ended, there would be redemption and a return to the homeland and Jerusalem . . .

"In the third place, he does the same as other prophets, and prophesies about Christ and His kingdom, especially in Chapters 23 and 31, where he clearly speaks of Christ, of His kingdom, of the New Testament and the end of the Old Testament . . .

"The same conditions prevail everywhere today. Now that the end of the world approaches, people everywhere rage and storm against God most horribly. They blaspheme and condemn God's Word, which they consciously recognize as God's Word and the truth. Besides, there are so many fearful signs and wonders, both in the heavens and nearly everywhere in creation, to frighten men. The times are as evil and distressful as those of Jeremiah, and even worse.

"But it will and must be so, that people become secure and cry: Peace, there is no need to worry! They abuse everything God wants, and ignore every threat until (as St. Paul says) perdition suddenly overtakes and destroys them before they realize it.

"And yet Christ knows how to preserve His people. For their sakes He lets His Word shine in these terrible times, as He preserved Daniel and his friends. For their sakes the prophecy of Jeremiah had to shine forth" (*Die Deutsche Bibel* [Luther's German translation of the Bible], vol. 11.1, author's translation [Weimar: Hermann Böhlau, 1960), 190–95).

125. This can well serve as a summation of the book. Suggest your own way of putting it all together.

126. Jeremiah spoke in great detail about the sins of Judah (e.g., 2:4–13; 3:1–10; 5:1–9, 23–31; 6:16–19; 7:1–18, 30–31; 8:4–12, 19; 9:2–8; 10:2–9; 17:1–13; 18:18; 19:4–5, 13; and 20:1–6). Could one go about our land and make a similar group of accusations? If so, what message might accompany the accusations?

127. The words of 23:1–8 were fulfilled in Jesus (see John 10). What value do these words have for Christians today?

128. Have you heard people say, in effect, "Peace, there is no need to worry"? How would Jeremiah respond to these words? What does Jesus say in Matthew 10:34?

129. Share passages that were particularly meaningful to you. Which passages in Jeremiah would you select for further study and explanation?

130. At this point, what is your personal impression of the Book of Jeremiah? Do you like the book? Is there too much anger and denunciation in it? How would you use it?

131. How does Jeremiah's life and message both serve to underline our need for a Savior and illuminate the life and work of Jesus Christ for us?

When the Book of Jeremiah first appeared, it was cut to pieces and burned (ch. 36)! It was rewritten and is now a book of the Bible more than twenty-five hundred years old. It is a precious book, giving rich reward for the faith and life of every thoughtful reader.

Jeremiah speaks the Word of the Lord to us today. God pronounces judgment against the evil reflected in the social, political, and economic arenas of life. Yet God also proclaims a rich message of hope and encouragement for us to live as sojourners in the world while sharing the Gospel of salvation in Christ Jesus.

As a result of this study, may the Holy Spirit lead you to better appreciate the life and work of Jesus and the mission to which you have been called.

Close with prayer.

Leader Notes

Preparing to Teach Jeremiah and Lamentations

To prepare to lead this study, read through the Books of Jeremiah and Lamentations. Concentrate on the prose sections in Jeremiah, which reveal the life of the prophet. You might secure a good commentary on the book and read it over or read the introduction to the book in *The Concordia Self-Study Bible* or a Bible handbook. A reading of 1 Kings 22–25 would also be helpful as background. Several maps of the Old Testament world at about 600 B.C. would also help, especially with the first three lessons.

The Leader notes are provided as a "safety net," a place to turn for help in answering questions and for enriching discussion. They will not answer every question raised in your class. Please read them, along with the questions, before class. Consult it in class only after exploring the Bible references and discussing what they teach. Please note the different abilities of your class members. Some will easily find the Bible passages listed in this study; others will struggle. To make participation easier, team up members of the class. For example, if a question asks you to look up several passages, assign one passage to one group, the second to another, and so on. Divide the work! Let participants present the answers they discover.

If you have the opportunity, you will find it helpful to make use of other biblical reference works in the course of your study. These two commentaries can be very helpful: Theodore Laetsch, *Jeremiah*, Concordia Classic Commentary Series (St. Louis: Concordia Publishing House, 1952) and David M. Gosdeck, *Jeremiah/Lamentations*, People's Bible Commentary (Milwaukee: Northwestern Publishing House, 1994; reprinted by Concordia Publishing House, 1995). Although it is not strictly a commentary, the section on Jeremiah in *The Word Becoming Flesh* by Horace Hummel (St. Louis: Concordia Publishing House, 1979) also contains much that is of value for the proper interpretation of this biblical book.

Group Bible Study

Group Bible study means mutual learning from one another under the guidance of a leader. The Bible is an inexhaustible resource. No one person can discover all it has to offer. In a class many eyes see many things and can apply them to many life situations. As the leader, you should resist the temptation to "give the answers" and so act as an "authority." This teaching approach stifles participation by individual members and can actually hamper learning. As a general rule the teacher is not to *give* interpretation but to *develop* interpreters. Of course there are times when you should and must share insights and information gained by your study and by your class members through the lesson. And you'll want to engage class members in meaningful sharing and discussion at all points, leading them to a summary of the lesson at the close. As a general rule, don't explain what the learners can discover by themselves.

Have a chalkboard and chalk or newsprint and marker available to emphasize significant points of the lesson. Rephrase your inquiries or the inquiries of participants as questions, problems, or issues. This provokes thought. Keep discussion to the point. List on the chalkboard or newsprint the answers given. Then determine the most vital points made in the discussion. Ask additional questions to fill gaps.

The aim of every Bible study is to help people grow spiritually, not merely in biblical and theological knowledge, but in Christian thinking and living. This means growth in Christian attitudes, insights, and skills for Christian living. The focus of this course must be the church and the world of our day. The guiding question will be this: What does the Lord teach us for life today through the prophet Jeremiah?

Teaching the Old Testament

Teaching the Old Testament can degenerate into mere moralizing in which do-goodism becomes a substitute for the Gospel and sanctification gets confused with justification. Actually the justified sinner is not moved by Law but by God's grace to a totally new life. His or her faith in Christ is always at work in every context of life. Meaningful personal Christianity consists of faith flowing from God's grace and is evidenced in love for other people. Having experienced God's free grace and forgiveness, the Christian daily works in his or her world to reflect the will of God for humanity in every area of human endeavor.

The Christian leader is Gospel oriented, not Law oriented. He or she distinguishes Law from Gospel. Both are needed. There is no clear Gospel unless we first have been crushed by the Law and see our sinfulness. There is no genuine Christianity where faith is not followed by life pleasing to God. In fact, genuine faith is inseparable from life. The Gospel alone creates in us the new heart that causes us to love God and our neighbor.

When Christians teach the Old Testament, they do not teach it as a "law book," but instead as books containing both Law and Gospel. They see the God of the Old Testament as a God of grace who out of love establishes a covenant of love with His people (Deuteronomy 7:6–9) and forgives their sins. Christians interpret the Old Testament using the New Testament message of fulfilled prophecy through Jesus Christ. They teach as leaders who personally know the Lord Jesus as Savior, the victorious Christ who gives all believers a new life (2 Corinthians 5:17) and a new mission (John 20:21).

Pace Your Teaching

The lessons in this course of study are designed for a study session of at least an hour in length. If it is the desire and intent of the class to complete an entire lesson each session, it will be necessary for you to summarize the content of certain answers or biblical references in order to preserve time. Asking various class members to look up different Bible passages and to read them aloud to the rest of the class will save time over having every class member look up each reference.

Also, you may not want to cover every question in each lesson. Be selective. Pace your teaching. Spend no more than 5–10 minutes opening the lesson. During the lesson, get the sweep of meaning. Occasionally stop to help the class gain understanding of a word or concept. Allow approximately 5 minutes for closing the lesson and announcements.

Should your group have more than a one-hour class period, you can take it more leisurely. But do not allow any lesson to drag and become tiresome. Keep it moving. Keep it alive. Keep it meaningful. Eliminate some questions and restrict yourself to those questions most meaningful to the members of the class. If most members study the text at home, they can report their findings, and the time gained can be applied to relating the lesson to life.

Good Preparation

Good preparation by you, the leader, usually affects the pleasure and satisfaction the class will experience.

Suggestions to the Leader for Using the Study Guide

The Lesson Pattern

This set of lessons is designed to aid *Bible study*, that is, to aid a consideration of the written Word of God, with discussion and personal application growing out of the text at hand.

The typical lesson is divided into these sections:
1. Theme Verse
2. Objectives
3. Questions and Answers
4. Closing

The theme verse and objectives give you assistance in arousing the interest of the group in the concepts of the lesson. Here is where you stimulate minds of the class members. Do not linger too long over the introductory remarks.

The questions and answers provide the real spadework necessary for Bible study. Here the class digs, uncovers, and discovers; it gets the facts and observes them. Your comments are needed only to the extent that they help the group understand the text. The questions in this guide, corresponding to sections within the text, are intended to help the participants discover the meaning of the text.

Having determined what the text says, the class is ready to apply the message. Having heard, read, marked, and learned the Word of God, proceed to digest it inwardly through discussion, evaluation, and application. This is done, as this guide suggests, by taking the truths found in Scripture and applying them to the world and Christianity in general and then to personal Christian life. Class time may not permit discussion of all questions and topics. In preparation you may need to select one or two and focus on them. Close the session by reviewing one important truth from the lesson.

Remember, the Word of God is sacred, but this Study Guide is not. The notes in this section offer only guidelines and suggestions. Do not hesitate to alter the guidelines or substitute others to meet your needs and the needs of the participants. Adapt your teaching plan to your class and your class period. Good teaching directs the learner to discover for himself or herself. For you, the teacher, this means directing the learner, not giving the learner answers. Choose the verses that should be looked up in Scripture. What discussion questions will you ask? At what points? Write them in the margin of your Study Guide. Involve class members, but give them clear directions. What practical actions might you propose for the week following the lesson? Which of the items do you consider most important for your class?

How will you best use your teaching period? Do you have 45 minutes? an hour? or an hour and a half? If time is short, what should you cut? Learn to become a wise steward of class time.

Be sure to take time to summarize the lesson, or have a class member do it. Plan a brief opening devotion, using members of the class.

Remember to pray frequently for yourself and your class. May God the Holy Spirit bless your study and your leading of others into the comforting truths of God's Christ-centered Word.

Lesson 1

The Prophet's Work

Theme verse: *"Before I formed you in the womb I knew you, before you were born I set you apart; I appointed you as a prophet to the nations."*

Jeremiah 1:5

Objectives

By the power of the Holy Spirit working through God's Word, we will

- understand what a prophet is;
- learn what God called a prophet to do;
- support God's spokesmen today;
- speak God's Word to our family, friends, and neighbors.

1. Help the class members recognize that Scripture speaks of a prophet as (a) a leader in religious life, a general activity; (b) a revealer of the unknown, a specific ability; and (c) a proclaimer of the Word, the essential task.

Not all the passages illustrating the use of the word *prophet* need to be read by all class members. You might divide the class into small groups and ask each group to respond to one or two readings. Take time for the groups to share their findings and to react to the ways in which the term is used. Emphasize that the word *prophet* or *prophecy* was used for fortune-telling and also as a designation for a spiritual leader—a teacher. Then move on to the final paragraph in this section, which deals with the specific concept of *prophet* important for this study.

Place special emphasis on speech and proclamation. It was his preaching that immediately marked John the Baptist as a prophet, and

Jesus was the great prophet because of His calling to "preach" the Kingdom (Matthew 4:17).

2. As the class pages through the books of the prophets, if no one discovers the answer, indicate that it is the length of the first four that make them "major," not their priority or importance.

3. List challenges. God also calls us to speak for Him.

4. Speaking for God, symbolism, and vision.

Help the class to see the increased prophetic activity during the Old Testament. Ask them to suggest possible reasons for the changes in the ways that God used prophets. Lead them to see the various problems that the prophets faced during different periods of history.

5. Jesus Christ remains the greatest of all the prophets. His ministry combined all of the prophets' functions. He taught, told the future, spoke for God. Let the class give examples. More than this, He was not only the Messenger, but the Message as well, proclaiming Himself as the Son of God and Savior of the world. Ask the class to give examples from His life that illustrate this fact.

6. Read as many of the passages aloud as you have time for. The prophetic office was given to all of the apostles and followers of the Lord, to Timothy and the church of his day. Although God does not call all of us to be prophets, He calls all of us to speak His Word.

7. Answers may vary. The task of the prophetic church today is not merely to preach about Jesus Christ, but actually to preach Him (1 Corinthians 1:23; 2:1–2). These words of Paul are the measure of the church and determine the church's final success or failure.

These additional questions might stimulate discussion in your group:

a. What is the business of the church? Does it include social, educational, and cultural responsibilities? On a scale of values, where does the task of proclaiming the Gospel belong on the list of church functions?

b. How do we actually measure up to that?

c. What can we do to be more effective prophets to one another? to others?

Lesson 2

The World of Jeremiah

Theme verse: *Then the king called together all the elders of Judah and Jerusalem. He went up to the temple of the LORD with the men of Judah, the people of Jerusalem, the priests and the prophets—all the people from the least to the greatest. He read in their hearing all the words of the Book of the Covenant, which had been found in the temple of the LORD.*

2 Kings 23:1–2

Objectives

By the power of the Holy Spirit working through God's Word, we will

- understand the setting of Jeremiah's prophetic ministry;
- apply God's Word in our national and personal setting.

Read over 2 Kings 22–25 again and read 2 Chronicles 34–36 as background. If you can obtain a copy of *A History of Israel* by John Bright (Philadelphia: Westminster John Knox Press, 2000), a reading of Chapter 8, "The Kingdom of Judah," would be of help.

8. Read through portions of 1 Kings 11:43–12:20 you have selected for the class. 1 Kings describes the division of Israel into northern and southern kingdoms. Emphasize the detrimental effect of the division. The remainder of the lesson will highlight some of the difficulties. Use the map on p. 109 to show the division.

9. Causes included (a) worshiping foreign gods, (b) following the practices of other nations, and (c) neglecting God's Word and the preaching of the prophets. The author of 2 Kings emphasizes spiritual and moral causes rather than economic or political causes.

The reference in 2 Kings 17:7–19 shows that God, in His time, does mete out the consequences of sin to a nation. Repentance, not alliances with other nations, could have saved the nation of Judah.

10. The changing political situation in ancient times could remind one of the rise and fall of world powers such as Nazi Germany, the Soviet Union, and the British Empire. Nations such as Japan and China have likewise collapsed but reemerged with new strength. Just as maps and alliances constantly shifted for ancient Israel, so they continue to change today.

11. Judah should have recognized the weakness of worldly political alliances. The Lord calls them to faithfulness, not just good policy.

12. Answers will vary.

13. By their own strength, the people of Judah were powerless to resist such mighty empires as Babylon. God had promised to protect and preserve them, but they continually adopted the corrupt ways and beliefs of their neighbors.

14. Refer to the chronology of events in the opening pages of this guide for additional information about the times of Jeremiah. You might divide the class into five groups and ask each to find some information about each king. If you are short of time, assign this section for research at home. Talk about the burden of Jeremiah as God's prophet in that difficult, violent age.

15. This is an opportune time to work with the map of the lands of Jeremiah. If you have the facilities, prepare an overhead transparency of the map in the back pages and then an overlay of the same area in today's history with the identification of modern geographical and political designations.

In ancient times, the area northeast from Egypt to the Euphrates River and then southeast to the Persian Gulf was known as the Fertile Crescent, as distinguished from the vast desert regions of Arabia. It was desirable territory and therefore the object of international conflict. Today the oil of the desert is a comparable prize and gives a new dimension to the struggle.

The size of Judah was about 95 miles by 45 miles, less than half the size of Vermont, only a very small link in the chain of nations along the Fertile Crescent. But it was vital for commercial and military movement of world powers, and therefore was subject to constant tension. It held a position not unlike that of the smaller nations of the

Middle East today, and became similarly involved in international intrigue and conflict.

Note: There is a view of history that pictures world events as happening on a continuous circle, that "history repeats itself." Perhaps it is better to see these events in a spiral motion, not simply a meaningless repetition but a movement toward a point determined by the Lord of all history.

16. As long as God's people are in the world, they are influenced by world events. In turn, they likewise make their impact on human history. The age of discovery and world exploration saw empire, commerce, and the church move hand in hand in the search for new lands to claim for their separate interests. The cross and the national standard were often planted side by side on new shores. Each has had an effect on the other in the developments that then followed.

Use these thoughts as door openers for discussion: Freedom of worship in U.S. churches was inseparable from political independence. Moral and ethical standards of the church helped establish ordinances and customs of secular life and are today, in turn, responding to the pressures of the world outside the church. (Think of what has happened, e.g., to the status of Sunday since Puritan days or to attitudes toward home and family.)

17. Look for honest input. Don't just concentrate on the negatives. What can we contribute in the conflict of our time? What power and help do we have? How can we encourage one another?

Lesson 3

The Life and Character of Jeremiah

Theme verse: *But the LORD said to me, "Do not say, 'I am only a child.' You must go to everyone I send you to and say whatever I command you. Do not be afraid of them, for I am with you and will rescue you," declares the LORD.*

Jeremiah 1:7–8

Objectives

By the power of the Holy Spirit working through God's Word, we will

- learn about Jeremiah's background and calling;
- understand His struggle and strength as a prophet;
- grow in faithful persistence.

Before class read over the suggested portions of Scripture and the summary of Jeremiah's life in the Study Guide. If possible, read over a study Bible or Bible handbook summary as preparation.

Read 1:1–8 in connection with the opening paragraphs. Ask class members to put themselves in Jeremiah's place.

18. Answers will vary. Jeremiah's struggles exceed the struggles that most of us experience today.

19. It is not necessary for every class member to read every reference. You may select a few representative passages or divide the passages among individuals or groups and ask them to share what they find. All the passages give evidence of the tension that existed between Jeremiah and many of his countrymen.

20. God was leading Jeremiah to place full reliance on Him as the One who would provide both the strength and the message. The vision of the almond branch strengthened this reliance. The branch of the almond was the first evidence of new life in the spring. It afforded Jeremiah the surety for the speedy and certain fulfillment of the message he was to proclaim. This confidence certainly was necessary in the face of the vision of the boiling pot, the catastrophe from Babylon, which set the scene for one of the major themes of the book.

21. Assign the Scripture portions to groups. Ask for a brief report on each reluctant prophet (Moses, Gideon, Isaiah). Then let the class suggest others (Jonah, Balaam, etc.). Emphasize that God's promised presence with us in Jesus (Matthew 28:20) is our encouragement and power to overcome our own reluctance to follow.

22. Answers will vary. The "noble army of martyrs" (Te Deum, Order of Matins) have suffered for their faith. A few names could include Daniel, Peter, John, Paul, Luther, and Bonhöffer. The passage from Hebrews is a eulogy to their memory. The purpose of this record was not merely a grateful remembrance. It serves also as an inspiration to all the generations of the church.

23. God has not promised His servants a garden of roses. Note that in His words the hardship is imposed by those outside the true church, where it might easily be expected. If there is no persecution, if Christians suffer no response to their teaching, they may be hiding their witness and rejecting their call to speak God's message.

If the Christian ministry were a glamorous profession, there would be long lines of applicants for the work. It was never meant to be such a profession. But that does not give God's people the right to make the ministry more burdensome than it already is. What can we do to promote recruitment for church professions?

24. Such recruitment efforts probably would not appeal to people today. We are so comfortable and have so many other opportunities.

25. If possible, show a picture of Michelangelo's portrayal of Jeremiah (check the Internet). Ask for reactions. Like Jeremiah, Christians today still depend upon the Gospel for support in bearing their burdens.

26. Examples abound. Receive the group's answers and ask members to consider which expressions are most striking to them.

27. Jeremiah knew he faced the worst possible obstacles. He also knew God would overcome them. Sometimes God's people don't get

the opportunity to see the promised victory. But no matter what we suffer, we share in Christ's victory and inherit the kingdom of God.

Lesson 4

Early Prophecies

Theme verse: *Go, proclaim this message toward the north: "Return, faithless Israel," declares the LORD, "I will frown on you no longer, for I am merciful," declares the LORD, "I will not be angry forever. Only acknowledge your guilt."*

Jeremiah 3:12–13

Objectives

By the power of the Holy Spirit working through God's Word, we will

- begin to study God's revelations to Jeremiah;
- reflect on our calling to proclaim both Law and Gospel in the church and society;
- pray for wisdom to apply God's Word today.

Read over the lesson in the Study Guide and the portions of Scripture indicated. Mark passages that seem important to be read in class.

Review briefly the historical setting from Lesson 2. Discuss also the spiritual depravity that led to the downfall of the nation. This lesson focuses upon the state of wickedness that existed.

Some of the majesty of Jeremiah's poetry is contained in the sections under study here. Some of them could be read aloud, dramatically, in class.

In each section read through the passage first, then the Study Guide summary. Use the questions for discussion.

28. The futility of false religion is clear from 2:13. By way of contrast, see Isaiah 55:1; Revelation 21:6; and 22:17. The enduring

nature of sin (2:22) shows the need for God's grace (Isaiah 1:18). Note the effective use of accusing questions in this section—2:5, 11, 14, 17–18, 23, 28–29, 31; 3:1.

29. Jeremiah may have had a part in Josiah's reform. This is nowhere clearly determined. Later, however, the prophet declares the failure of that movement to have lasting effect on the people. See 6:16–21; 7:1–15.

30. The church must certainly proclaim the Law of God (e.g., Ezekiel 33:1–9). But since people cannot keep the Law, the Gospel must be heard unmistakably loud and clear. Otherwise, no one will receive God's salvation.

31. The Gospel is not merely any good news for any bad situation. It is the message of the grace of God in Jesus Christ. Most specifically, the Gospel teaches that Jesus Christ died for the forgiveness of our sins and rose to be our Savior. The Law is God's statement of His requirements for us. Alone, the Law leads us to despair because we cannot meet God's standard of perfection. The Gospel is the good news that God has acted for us in Jesus Christ, who kept the Law and brings us back into fellowship with God by His forgiveness.

32. The chief purpose of the Law is to reveal people's sins and drive them to repentance. The Law prepares people to receive the blessings of the Gospel.

33. The words of 5:23–29 remain an indictment of the world in all the ages. The world today says, "It is a dog-eat-dog existence, and any way to make a buck is all right. We want to get ahead no matter whom we trample in the process." Can the class give examples from their own experience or observation? Philippians 2:4 describes how God's people should act differently.

34. Answers will vary. Consider what happens to Christian principles when a promotion is at stake. Christians should be concerned about the well-being of others (1 John 4:7–11). Perhaps we fail to love others because we fail to appreciate God's love for us.

35. Jeremiah overlooks no one in his accusation, neither the spiritual leaders nor the people. All are involved. But ultimately he blames the leaders (ch. 25; 50:6).

36. Answers will vary. Who is to blame for the evil in our world and the crime in our streets? Is it our government, our laws, our courts, our homes, our educational system, or the organized church? To what

84

extent do we shape these forces by our own reluctance to do right and to accept the consequences of our wrong? Modern democracy places greater responsibility for right and wrong on the individuals, since they choose their leaders and even make policy decisions through referenda. In the church, are we really willing to accept and observe what the Lord says to us through His messengers today? Or are we perhaps resentful toward the truth and secretly glad when our own sore spots are not irritated? At times Christians may encourage God's prophets to water down the message and tell us what we want to hear rather than what we need to hear. Sometimes the sheep insist on leading the shepherd.

Lesson 5

The Temple Message

Theme verse: *I know, O LORD, that a man's life is not his own; it is not for man to direct his steps. Correct me, LORD, but only with justice—not in Your anger, lest You reduce me to nothing.*

Jeremiah 10:23–24

Objectives

By the power of the Holy Spirit working through God's Word, we will

- investigate the temple sermons of Jeremiah;
- understand ancient and modern forms of idolatry;
- confess the Lord as our only Savior.

Discuss the visible evidences of idolatry suggested in 7:16–20. Note that the Queen of Heaven (7:18) is not the mother of our Lord, but Ishtar (Astarte), the goddess of fertility and sensuous lover in a number of ancient pagan religious systems. Chapter 44 indicates that little heed had been taken of Jeremiah's earlier message.

37. The record in 2 Kings 22–23 and in 2 Chronicles 34–35 speaks of the reform in glowing terms and praises Josiah as a veritable saint (2 Kings 23:25). But the reformation seems to have had only an outward effect on the people, who actually did not change but persisted in their former wickedness.

38. The people were confident that they were blessed because they maintained the Lord's house. Today we might say that they were members of the "right church" but had failed to receive its teaching. See Joel 2:12–13 and Isaiah 1:11–17.

39. This quote may help your discussion: "Placing one's trust in the possession of orthodoxy received by tradition from the fathers, or in the correctness of ritualistic forms, or in the prayers one speaks, or

in the services attended, or in the offerings given, is in God's sight a form of idolatry, no matter whether committed in Judah or in America, by Jews or pagans or Lutherans, and is the same abomination to the Lord . . . and will meet with the same judgment that came upon Israel and Judah" (Laetsch, p. 96).

The point of the discussion should not be just to find fault with the church or an individual congregation. Talk about ways in which the church can guard against "empty" religious practices. Try to make a list of practical suggestions.

40. If the world were to judge the value of the Gospel by your attitudes and actions toward other people, what would the verdict be? Read 2 Corinthians 3:2–3 as you discuss this issue. To take this seriously may mean to lose some advantage or profit. Try to talk honestly about our difficulty in maintaining our priorities.

41. There was a time when people depended directly on one another for their well-being. The welfare state tends to depersonalize concern for others. Our responsibility to our neighbors gets handled by an agency. This hinders the exercise of the Christian life of service and witness. Relate Matthew 25:31–46 to your discussion. Consider how we can effectively deal with both the mass of humanity and each individual.

42. Discuss the purpose of worship and of the church. Note that Jesus does not simply drive out the money changers. He urges prayer, shows mercy, and welcomes genuine worship.

43. This question is not aimed at the quality of today's preaching. Avoid sermon critiques here. Stick to the point of the passages. The question suggests honest self-examination. Do we perhaps have situations today that would call for a "temple sermon"? What conditions, if any, among us might have aroused the wrath of Jeremiah and of Jesus? Reflect on the role of the Law, the Gospel, and patience in bringing about changes at church.

44. No time in history has been without its idols. Today is certainly no exception. Lead the class to list current idolatry that disturbs them most. The lessons of repentance have not been passed on to the next generation. The people are making the same mistakes.

45. Christians should be distinguishable by their lifestyle, as stated in Romans 12:2. That includes not merely their good works (Matthew 5:16), but also their rejection of evil works (Philippians 2:15). Only the Holy Spirit can bring about this transformation.

46. Let the class evaluate statements like these: "Everybody's doing it" (social pressure). "It can't be wrong when it seems so right" (flexible conscience). "I must do these things to get ahead" (personal gain). Because Christ gave His life for us, we may now give our lives for others (2 Corinthians 5:14–15).

47. The questions show the foolishness of the people's actions and God's frustration with them. Their hearts remain hardened to God's commands. Now God will not turn from punishing them.

48. Answers will vary. Note that God provides for the forgiveness of all sins and graciously calls all people to repentance. However, as the Book of Jeremiah demonstrates, God does get frustrated with unrepentance. In faith, we can see His discipline/punishment as an expression of fatherly love and concern (Hebrews 12:5–11).

49. Apparently the scribes had failed to make copies of the "Book of the Law" available for the rulers or for people in general. Their "lying pen" was either idle or put to use copying something other than God's Word.

50. Answers will vary. Consider the Bible-study opportunities at your congregation, whether your services focus on God's Word, and how you encourage study of Scripture in people's homes. In particular, consider whether parents and children are reading Bible stories together at home.

51. 1 Kings 4:29–34 contrasts King Solomon's divinely inspired wisdom with the wisdom of other nations. The ancient Israelites were aware of the literature of other people, and God did not forbid them to read such texts. For example, the section in Proverbs called "Saying of the Wise" (22:17) shows strong correspondence with the Egyptian "Wisdom of Amenemope." However, the scribes of Jeremiah's day had placed too great an emphasis on studying other "wisdom" and neglected the only firm and reliable source of wisdom: God's Word.

52. The leaders and the people are shameless in their sin. As a result, God will completely humiliate them.

53. Shame has its place in changing people's behavior. However, goodness does not come from shame but from a changed heart and a sincere desire to please God. Shame is the result of the Law or fear. Goodness comes as a gift from God through the Gospel.

54. The Lord had not utterly forsaken Zion. In fact He had not utterly forsaken Israel, the Northern Kingdom. Even as the people went into exile, God planned their restoration.

55. Answers will vary. Most Christians experience times when the Lord seems intimate or distant. Note as you read Jeremiah how often God complains that the people have "forsaken" Him. God, too, feels our rejection and distance (Jeremiah 17:13; 19:4). The Lamentations passage shows how Jeremiah felt forsaken by God but continued to pray for restoration. Recall Jesus' words from the cross (Mark 15:33–34), His prayer (Luke 23:46), and how the heavenly Father restored His life.

56. The Lord did have healing for the people but, like a wise and patient doctor, He would apply the healing at the proper time. He will do the same for you through Christ, the Healer.

57. Answers will vary. Given the either/or choice between earthly wisdom, might, and riches on the one hand and saving faith with all its gifts on the other—honestly now, which would you choose? Which of these presents the greatest temptation for you?

58. Answers will vary. Have the class list 10 people they would call great. Read 1 Samuel 16:7 and Matthew 20:25–28. Would they make any changes on their list?

59. In matters of national security, the struggle between doves and hawks will continue, and human leadership is responsible to God for honest and considered judgments and decisions. Faith has its own approach to the questions involved. Faith knows and accepts Psalm 33:16–17; 118:8–9; 127:1–2. Faith also prays with confidence the Lord's Prayer. Yet, as the Nehemiah passage shows, trust in the Lord (4:16–23) does not mean we lay down our arms. God calls us to both faith and action.

60. There is a difference between knowing about God and knowing Him. It is the difference between intellect and faith. The first is necessary, but the second is salvation. We may know much about a noted or even notorious person, with no benefit to us. Knowledge with blessing is life (Philippians 3:7–11).

61. For this activity it will be helpful if you are able to use a chalkboard, a large sheet of paper, an overhead projector, or some similar visual aid. If these are not available, you might ask class members to write the items that they suggest. Examine the listing. Idols cannot speak, walk, harm, or do good. They are created; they cannot create. They will perish. They bring shame, have no breath, and no worth. The Lord speaks, is unique, and is powerful. He rules and deserves worship. He is the true, living, eternal King. When He gets

angry, the nations cannot endure. The Lord made the world with power, wisdom, and understanding. Creation responds to Him, the "Portion of Jacob" and "Maker of all things."

62. Answers will vary. Is unbelief any more than foolishness, a refusal to accept the clear words of God?

Lesson 6

The Covenant and
the Potter's Wheel

Theme verse: *If at any time I announce that a nation or kingdom is to be uprooted, torn down and destroyed, and if that nation I warned repents of its evil, then I will relent and not inflict on it the disaster I had planned.*

Jeremiah 18:7–8

Objectives

By the power of the Holy Spirit working through God's Word, we will

- learn about the covenant and its obligations;
- pray that the Lord would mold and shape our lives according to His design;
- comfort and encourage those who wrestle with depression or personal failure.

63. Answers will vary. The passages point to the following means by which idolatry can enter people's lives: failing to heed God's Word, following evil hearts, repeating the sins of earlier generations, conspiring to do evil though continuing in worship.

64. We are not just talking about worshiping little statues—but the temptation to put ourselves and our needs and wants in the place of God. Ask yourselves, what is most important to you? How can health, social concerns, success in business, leisure, creature comforts, or sex become the focus of our existence? In the church, could the worship of organizations, efficiency, law and order, political power, and peace at any price qualify as idolatry?

65. The point is that if anything, even though it may in itself be permissible and even desirable, becomes more important to us than

God Himself, then Jeremiah's message applies to us. Lord, have mercy upon us!

66. Consider in what kinds of settings parents might say, "That's my daughter" or "That's my son." Talk about the implications of, and the comfort we can find in God's calling us His people.

67. The key to Jeremiah is in 19:11—total destruction beyond repair. Second Timothy shows that God's people have a variety of gifts, some impressive in our judgment, others insignificant. But by God's grace all are serviceable and useful. (For a similar thought, see Zechariah 14:20–21.) Second Corinthians shows that the important thing is the treasure and not the container, the gift and not the wrappings. This is a word of warning not to despise the messenger of the Gospel. But what a word of comfort and encouragement to the messenger! (See 1 Corinthians 15:9–10 and 1 Timothy 1:12–17.)

68. Encourage personal answers. Certainly faith implies both a complete trust in God and a faithful response from the believer.

69. Jeremiah wishes he had never been born at all. It becomes a death wish.

70. We exist because God permitted us to have life. We can trust that His will is being accomplished in our lives even when we feel like utter failures or wish that life was over. Note the hope of Paul. He felt himself ready for the rest of heaven, yet he clung to the belief that God still had service for him in this life.

71. Jeremiah 20:11–13 reveals the prophet's faith mixed with frustration. Jeremiah could always go back to his calling when he struggled with depression and doubt. In a similar way, a Christian can return to his or her Baptism and find a blessing from God that never wears out. God has placed His name on You, CHRISTian. The devil, the world, and your own sin cannot blot that name out!

72. There are many Jeremiahs today. Pastors and teachers are truly human. They are aware of their failures. They are sometimes unfairly criticized and condemned. They need the understanding love of their people and every encouragement we can give them. Again, list positive, practical ways of encouraging and helping God's servants among you.

73. We must often struggle with the temptation to speak pious words without the deep trust that really depends upon God to direct the affairs of our world. Though all earthly shepherds fail us, the heavenly Shepherd will never abandon His flock.

Lesson 7

The Exile

Theme verse: *"You will seek Me and find Me when you seek Me with all your heart. I will be found by you," declares the LORD.*

Jeremiah 29:13–14

Objectives

By the power of the Holy Spirit working through God's Word, we will
- understand the cause of the Babylonian captivity;
- grow in community service and outreach;
- make plans for the future in view of God's Word.

Read through 29:1–14 and the lesson in the Study Guide. Mark those passages that will be important to read in class. It would be helpful in beginning your discussion if you could bring some newspaper or magazine articles that deal with the persecution of dissenters in other countries. Use these to talk about our own response to aggression. Lead into your discussion of the biblical material.

Read through the biblical section and talk about life in captivity. Ask how we would accept sudden domination by some foreign power. Would we passively submit, or would we work for freedom?

74. As you seek to answer these questions, continue to try to place yourself into this situation or a similar situation today. Jeremiah's words were not likely very popular with the captives.

75. Answers will vary. To facilitate discussions set up a modern scenario such as the following: Communist China has overthrown your country and taken you to Beijing as a worker. Note how Jeremiah's counsel focuses on preserving the people and creating a future for them rather than on revenge through terrorism or guerrilla warfare.

76. The command of Jesus to be the salt of the earth and the light of the world has almost become a cliché. Use the example of Jeremiah to bring a deeper meaning to these words. Perhaps the class can think of some situations today in which it is just as difficult for Christians to be "salt" and "light" to those around them.

77. Discuss these in the light of encouragement of the Gospel and the forgiveness we need when we fail to live up to the standard of strength and visibility of faith we set for ourselves.

78. This is a good occasion to do an inventory of the activities of the congregation and/or its members in service to the human community. Think of elected or appointed political offices as well as of more voluntary participation in public education, family services, charitable groups, civic leadership, and the like. Think through the purpose of those activities; what part they play in our witness to our faith, in what sense they are "prophetic" activities, and what opportunities they offer for witnessing about Christ.

79. Jeremiah shows the way. Service to the community is one expression of faith. Like prayer, submission to government, honesty, and devotion to the home, community service is part of the Christian life and therefore should be encouraged by Christian leaders.

80. The blessings of God are earthly as well as spiritual. He can and does grant both blessings through the agency of His people. Examples: Christians in government who aim at justice and equity and the common good out of the inner conviction of the dignity of every individual as a redeemed creation of God, or who seek to exercise good stewardship of natural resources because these are the gifts of God.

81. Answers will vary.

82. Perhaps the classic example is that of Joseph in Egypt (Genesis 45:7–8; 50:19–20). Even Sodom and Gomorrah could have been spared if there had been as few as 10 righteous people there (Genesis 18:23–32).

83. Answers will vary. The following question includes Scripture references that will help participants form a Christ-like attitude toward government.

The goal for God's people is not to identify the ideal government under which the church exists and prospers. In fact, an "ideal" situation has its own built-in hazards of making God's people feel secure and lose the sense of the need of God or of reducing Christianity to a mere formalism, as in the instances where Christianity or a certain church were made state religions. Examples: the medieval church and modern state religions. By way of contrast, the times when Christianity was "at its best" were the times of persecution and hardship, as in the early church and the Reformation era. Today the church still lives under various hostile governments.

84. Jesus challenges us to pray as He prayed (Matthew 5:44; Luke 23:34). Paul urges Timothy and us to pray for health in body and mind, wisdom and sound judgment, a sense of justice and humanitarianism. Most of all, we should request knowledge of the truth and conversion to the Christian faith (Acts 26:28–29). See James 5:16.

85. He promises the following: He will come to them, fulfill His Word, and bring them home. He has plans for prosperity, hope, and a future. He will listen to their prayers and will be found by them.

86. Answers will vary. The Lord has great plans for you! In Christ He has created a future and a hope for each person and congregation that calls out to Him.

Lesson 8

The Book of Comfort

Theme verse: *"This is the covenant I will make with the house of Israel after that time," declares the* LORD. *" I will put My law in their minds and write it on their hearts. I will be their God, and they will be My people."*

Jeremiah 31:33

Objectives

By the power of the Holy Spirit working through God's Word, we will

- appreciate these chapters as the heart of Jeremiah's message;
- grow in good works based on the Gospel;
- sincerely repent of our sins and thank God for His new covenant in Christ.

Read over the entire "Book of Comfort," chapters 30–33, and get a feel for the magnificent expression of grace and hope there. Read through the lesson in the Study Guide, and mark those passages you will want to look up and discuss in class.

87. Let the class suggest passages before you offer these or others: Exodus 15:26; Isaiah 53:5; Hosea 6:1; Mark 2:17; Luke 4:18; and Revelation 22:2.

The image of God as the Great Healer is so meaningful for us because sickness is a universal experience, and sickness unto death is our common end. The parable brings God close to us. The transition from the physical to the spiritual is easily made. Jesus heals by teaching and by touch.

88. Jeremiah's words clearly show that Judah does not deserve to be restored. Then what moves God to promise restoration? It is His attitude toward mankind that is known as His grace, *His undeserved*

love toward mankind, perhaps the most important of all His qualities. Note how Paul makes grace and works mutually exclusive, Romans 11:5–6, and how he hammers that home in Ephesians 2:8–9. God's grace is the source of all His gifts, especially forgiveness, peace, and eternal life.

89. God works through His prophet toward restoration. Destruction is not an end in itself, but hopefully will be followed by reconstruction. There are times when the church must speak harshly, but its final purpose must always be the restoration of those who have fallen.

90. God calls us not just to act as moral critics or as the conscience of society but, what is most important, to build people up in the faith and plant the hope of the Gospel in their hearts.

91. Surprisingly many Christians believe God will still "count" our sins. But we are forgiven. Christ has fully paid our debt. We are no longer held accountable. The sins of believers are gone. They will not even be mentioned in the Judgment. (See 2 Corinthians 5:19.) Revelation speaks of God judging people based on what they have done (20:12–13). However, since the sins of God's people have been removed by Christ, the books against God's people are empty! (E.g., see the judgment described in Matthew 25:34–46.)

92. Matthew declares that the grief caused by Herod's slaughter of the innocents is a fulfillment of the Jeremiah passage and thus gives it a messianic meaning. Perhaps the connection between the two can be understood as follows: Both the suffering of God's Old Testament people and the death of the Bethlehem children caused deep mourning. Then the parallel could be extended to include Jeremiah 31:16–17 as implied in Matthew 2, namely, that God will establish through His Son, the Messiah, a new and better covenant. As Jeremiah prophesies a return of the exiles to their homeland, so God also promises that a day will come when His Messiah will preach peace to those who are far off and peace to those who are near (see Ephesians 2:17). In both cases, the hope of a better future life is the grace of God.

93. The passage contrasts the old covenant of Law—the unbearable yoke of bondage, which Israel broke again and again—and the new covenant of grace and forgiveness (see Acts 15:10 and Galatians 5:1). Now there is no need for repeated teaching to attain enough head knowledge about God to gain His approval. The knowledge of faith possesses all of God and makes the Christian a

partaker of all the total and complete fullness of His grace and salvation.

94. There are certainly hypocrites among church people. But this is no reason to reject the Gospel, which is intended for sinners only (Matthew 9:10–13). At the same time, we make no excuse for hypocrisy. The charge of Romans 2:17–24 is a serious one, which could be applied to people of the old covenant as well as the new.

95. The Letter to the Hebrews is intended to commend the Gospel of Jesus Christ to people of Jewish extraction. To quote from a prophet highly honored among the Jews was a convincing approach in the writer's efforts at persuasion.

96. The book is God's Word for Jesus and the apostles. This witness leads us likewise to honor it and to accept its validity for us.

97. Note God's answer to Jeremiah's question in verses 26–27. God's grace is always greater than our human sin. What He has done by His power is a sign and promise of what He can and will do in the days to come.

98. The exodus, the era of Elijah and Elisha (1 Kings 19; 2 Kings 6:8–20), the victory of the Gospel over legalism under Jesus and the apostles, and the restoration of the Gospel in the Reformation era are examples.

99. The critical word here is *church*. We use the word to mean "denomination" as well as the body of all who believe in Jesus Christ as Savior and Lord. See Acts 4:12; Acts 2:21; and Romans 10:13. Apart from the universal body of believers, there is no salvation. But no denomination can claim such a status.

100. This is an extension of the previous question. Do we have any assurance that human institutions, such as a synod or a local congregation, endure forever? Obviously not. Help point to the truth that the church endures forever because the believers, given eternal life in Jesus Christ, will endure forever.

101. Answers will vary. During an African famine, one hunger organization raised a vast sum of money solely for raising awareness of hunger—they sent virtually no aid!

102. The motivation behind an act is important. To give to another because it is expected is right—but to give to another because of God's love in Jesus Christ is best. Read Luke 6:32–36. To do good only because it pays is poor motivation.

103. The church cannot escape its responsibilities toward all people. It needs to help where help is needed (Galatians 6:10).

104. Answers will vary. The church has a responsibility to speak up for the oppressed and oppose wickedness (Proverbs 31:8–9).

105. (a) The church needs to speak out without fear or favor before all people, even those in high position. (b) Its message is often rejected, but God is still alive and well. (c) His Word and His promises still stand. (d) The Gospel will outlive every effort to silence it. See Psalm 46:10–11; Mark 13:31; and 1 Peter 1:24–25.

Note: Remind the class to submit the passage from Jeremiah for which further explanation is needed (see the closing section of Lesson 1). You need time to prepare your responses. The questions should be brought to the next class session.

Lesson 9

Lord of All the Nations

Theme verse: *A destroyer will come against Babylon; her warriors will be captured, and their bows will be broken.*

Jeremiah 51:56

Objectives

By the power of the Holy Spirit working through God's Word, we will

- learn about God's wrath and judgment;
- recognize God's control over national and international events;
- confess that the Lord governs our lives and future for our good.

Read over Jeremiah 25 and 46–51. As an opening exercise, before going to the Study Guide, you might write the word *jeremiad* on the board. Let the class suggest meanings. Can anyone think of modern jeremiads?

The destruction of Judah will be temporary. However, the vengeance of the Lord will fall with its full force upon the nations listed in 25:12–38.

106. Answers will vary.

107. In the midst of words of vengeance we find that our God is merciful (46:26b). He does provide a haven for His children and even for the descendants of those who oppressed Israel. He does keep His promises!

108. Class members undoubtedly will have knowledge of the sudden devastation brought about by a flash flood. Discuss how the prophecies of 47:2–4 are similar to the actions of people in the face of such a disaster.

109. Review the events that caused Ruth, from the land of Moab, to be listed in the genealogy of Jesus (Matthew 1:5). It seems that God is so merciful that He will bless an entire nation because of one individual.

110. People, as well as nations, have always attempted to act in such a way that future generations would place good connotations upon their names. But God sees fit that Babylon is not only destroyed, but that the term "Babylon" is used in Revelation as the very embodiment of all that is evil.

111. Ours is a world both bold and fearful. Technology seems omnipotent; it asks: Who needs God anymore? In poverty, we get help from the welfare agency. In sickness, we look to the miracle world of medicine and surgery. In anxiety, we go to the analyst. There are college courses designed to teach the acceptance of death. In international crises, we send the Secretary of State. And yet many people have never been as afraid as they are today. Psalm 24:1 still stands, in both its parts and in every sense of its claim.

112. The Lord is mighty to save but also to mete out judgment. Not even the church should expect to escape His chastisement (see Revelation 3:14–22).

113. Christ is "head over everything for the church" (Ephesians 1:22). Christ rules the world in the interest of the church. This section of Jeremiah should help us understand that God is still at the controls. We dare not try to take over His role and play God ourselves. At the same time, we must not be frightened as mighty powers rise and threaten to wipe out God's people (Luke 12:32). God has not promised Christians an easy life. But He does promise that His eternal plan will be completed in its smallest detail. No one and nothing can stand in His way (Matthew 16:18).

Lesson 10

Jeremiah and Jesus

Theme verse: *In the same way, after the supper He took the cup, saying, "This is the new covenant in My blood, which is poured out for you."*

Luke 22:20

Objectives

By the power of the Holy Spirit working through God's Word, we will

- note the similarities and differences between the ministries of Jesus and Jeremiah;
- confess the sinless sacrifice of Jesus Christ for the forgiveness of sins;
- receive the cup of the Lord's Supper as evidence that Jeremiah's prophecy of 31:31 is fulfilled.

After reading through the Study Guide, read through the passages suggested and make some notes about the comparisons suggested. As you read and review, you may be able to lengthen the list of similarities between Jesus and Jeremiah. Additional background for the comparison can be found in *Preaching from the Prophets* by Kyle M. Yates (Nashville: Broadman & Holman Publishers, 1991).

As you begin, it might be good to read the first paragraph and let the class members suggest similarities they have found in their study so far. Then move to the questions.

114. Babylon was on the verge of destroying Jerusalem during Jeremiah's day, while Rome was exercising rigid control during Jesus' time.

115. The class should see a clear rejection very early in the lives of both Jeremiah and Jesus.

116. While we do not know Jeremiah's age at the time of his call, the words "a child" (1:7) suggest that he was still relatively young, perhaps not much older than 12, the age at which Jesus accompanied His earthly parents to the temple.

117. The passages describe Jeremiah's constant struggle against the leaders of Jerusalem. Jesus, of course, faced constant controversy on His way to the cross.

118. Both references give evidence of the stranglehold that formalism had on Old Testament religion. Ask whether the class members see evidences of such formalism today. Consider how you can deal with the problem.

119. Emphasize the feeling both Jesus and Jeremiah had for the people. They "wept" for Jerusalem—for the lost people. Talk about the love of God in His "prophets" today that might cause us to "weep" over people.

120. Jeremiah may have been stoned to death by his countrymen in Egypt after he continued to speak of God's judgment upon them because of their sins (ch. 44). The comparisons with our Savior are obvious.

121. Very simply, Jeremiah was sinful and Jesus was without sin. In his sinful condition, it is likely that there were many instances when Jeremiah's thoughts, words, and deeds were in conflict with the will of God. The forgiveness of Jesus (Luke 23:34) shows up in sharp contrast with Jeremiah's desire for revenge (12:1–3 and 18:23).

122. Each of us responds in an individual way to our unique calling (1 Corinthians 12). Nevertheless, models of others can be an inspiration to us. You might discuss what it is that would enable us to be more like Jesus than like Jeremiah. Remember to remind the class of the forgiveness that is theirs when they succumb to temptation.

123. Answers will vary.

124. This question carries forward the incident of Matthew 16:13–14. Today Jesus holds the place of highest honor and is the ultimate criterion of all goodness. The thought of 1 Peter 2:12 applies here. Remember also John 13:34–35; 15:4–5, 8.

Lesson 11

A Summary of the Message

Theme verse: *I called on Your name, O LORD, from the depths of the pit. You heard my plea: "Do not close Your ears to my cry for relief." You came near when I called You, and You said, "Do not fear."*

Lamentations 3:55–57

Objectives

By the power of the Holy Spirit working through God's Word, we will

- review the message of Jeremiah;
- consider passages or questions of special interest;
- pray about the group's next topic of study.

At least two options are available for you as you discuss this lesson. You may wish to devote the entire session to discussing the questions submitted during Lesson 9, the key passages that class members brought to this session, or the material in the Study Guide. It might be good to make this decision before the class begins.

As you take up the questions submitted, don't be afraid to say, "I don't know." Perhaps you will need to meet with the class once more after you have researched some of the questions. Don't feel discouraged about not having mastered the book. No one else has. The study of the Word is a lifelong occupation. Thank God for that!

The key passages and the Study Guide materials may be studied on the basis of resources from the lessons. Encourage the class members to share their feelings and their faith with one another.

Read aloud the quote from Luther in the Study Guide. You may pause after each paragraph for discussion or talk about the entire section under Question 125.

The Study Guide questions are optional. Please do not feel bound by them. This is your class. With the Holy Spirit's guidance you, not the Study Guide or the Leader Notes, should control the nature and tone of the discussion.

125. Answers will vary.

126. Read over several of the passages—the ones you have chosen. Try to relate the conversation to our present day. Review any other portions of Jeremiah's words of judgment that seem to fit very well today. Talk about how they can be used.

127. Jesus becomes the "Good Shepherd" and calls Himself that. He laid down His life for us when He bled and died to take away our sins. He rose again to shepherd us all the days of our lives. Talk about the importance of the fulfillment and the comfort we can have through the assurance of Jesus' place as our Shepherd and Savior. You might ask the class for additional messianic prophecies they have found.

128. Summarize your discussion about the cost of living the Christian life. Discuss to what extent we can expect a peaceful life. If our life is peaceful, are we really serving and witnessing?

129. Encourage personal responses for the final questions and end the class with a clear witness to Jesus Christ, illuminated by the message of the prophet—the reason for our study of the book.

130. Answers will vary.

131. Answers will vary.

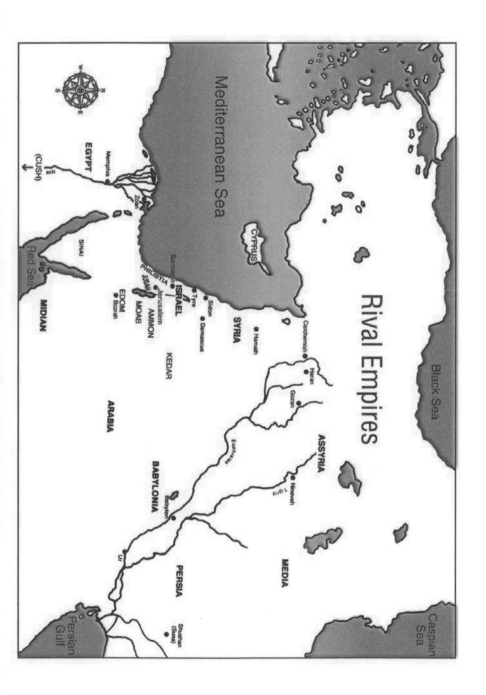

109